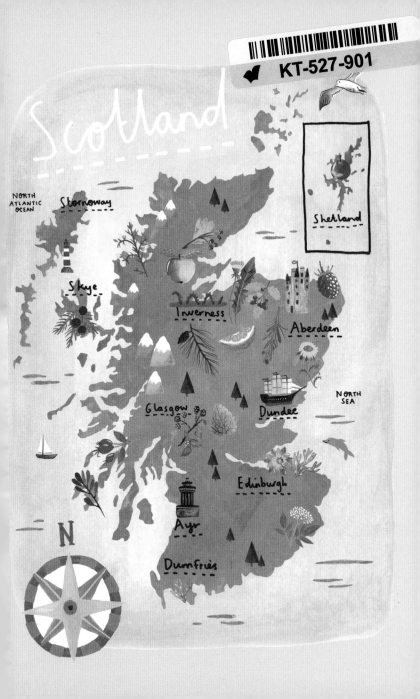

Scotland

NORTH
ATLANTIC
OCEAN

Stornoway

Skye

Inverness

Shetland

Aberdeen

NORTH
SEA

Glasgow

Dundee

Edinburgh

Ayr

Dumfries

N

GiN GALORE

A JOURNEY TO THE SOURCE OF
SCOTLAND'S GIN

Dedicated to all those people who are there
when distillers, gin producers and writers need a little
encouragement to keep working towards their goals.

First published 2018
by Black & White Publishing Ltd
Nautical House, 104 Commercial Street,
Edinburgh, EH6 6NF

1 3 5 7 9 10 8 6 5 4 2   18 19 20 21

ISBN: 978 1 78530 215 2

Design by Sue Rudge Design & Communication
Printed and bound in Turkey by Imago

Please drink responsibly.
www.drinkaware.co.uk

GiN
GALORE

A JOURNEY TO THE SOURCE OF
SCOTLAND'S GIN

SEAN MURPHY

BLACK & WHITE PUBLISHING

Contents

Introduction

THEY SAY THAT passion is infectious, and that all it takes is meeting the right person, in the right circumstances, to catch the bug. And that's what happened to me – first with whisky, and then with gin.

Scotland's fascination with distilling spirits has the intensity of a love affair that has lasted for centuries. Whisky is our country's number one export and our distillers are some of the most revered in the world.

However, in recent years, a different spirit has captured people's attention. There's been something of a gin renaissance – or a second gin craze, if you will – with more and more of us turning to the joys of a G&T, whether we're having a quiet night in at home, or heading out on the town. Scotland's producers have been quick on the uptake, taking inspiration from our rich distilling heritage to move into the production of gin. All over the country, from the Borders to the Shetland Isles, entrepreneurial producers have been creating a raft of excellent juniper spirits. From behind the bar to supermarket shelves, there has never been more choice. Scottish distilleries have turned to locally sourced plants, such as bog myrtle, bladderwrack seaweed and even the common garden nettle, giving them a new lease of life as botanical flavours in gin-making, and producing some of the most delicious and inventive new gins in the process.

In my days as a bartender, I was only familiar with brands like Bombay Sapphire and Gordon's, and viewed garnishes as a mild inconvenience. My fascination with this most versatile of spirits has grown and developed along with the industry itself. I was lucky enough to watch from the sidelines as the new gin craze took hold, and I knew I wanted to write about its impact in Scotland.

Each and every gin that you'll be introduced to in *Gin Galore* has its own story. I've chatted with producers from all over the country – from expert distillers with decades of experience, to talented newcomers who wanted to share their love of gin by making their own. I loved writing about – and sampling – each of the Scottish gins featured.

So, what makes a Scottish gin? This is something of a debate, perhaps because the gin category does not have the same kind of legislation that helped control the Scotch industry and give rise to the assertion of quality in whisky that is now lauded around the world. Though my fellow author Blair Bowman once described the Scottish craft gin sector as 'the Wild West', I'd liken it more to the Gold Rush – most producers are happy to do the hard work of actually getting into the mines to reach the gold, but there are a few who prefer to merely dip their toes in and gain their riches through panning on the outskirts . . .

Okay, that was a cluttered metaphor, but it helps to explain the current situation around the 'Scottish Gin' appellation – in this case the gold – as a definition of not only quality but also provenance and heritage. Most producers are based in Scotland and will distil their product here with botanicals – sometimes even the juniper berries – sourced locally in the region where the gin is made. However, there has been some confusion of late as to which brands are actually *made* in Scotland – and which are made elsewhere but given a 'Scottish Gin' label.

This book only includes gin makers who have a physical still – the vessel in which the magic happens! – in Scotland, or whose gin is made for them by a producer with one.

I've called the latter 'gin brands': this refers to those gins which are contract distilled (made by other distillers in Scotland), cuckoo distilled (created by the producers on someone else's still) or cold compound (a type of gin which sees flavours added to a base spirit without distillation) in Scotland. Those gins which are created by individual producers with their own Scottish still are simply titled 'gins'. These make up the majority of gins in *Gin Galore*.

The purpose of this book is to help you navigate the world of Scottish gins, to give you an idea of how each gin is made, who makes it, and how it reflects the area where is made. And, of course, how best to enjoy drinking it!

Most importantly, I hope that *Gin Galore* inspires you to get out there and try as many gins as you can and that, when offered the choice, you'll give a small-batch Scottish gin a try.

Jenever Juniper:
A History of Gin

FROM ANCIENT REMEDY to modern drinks superstar, the journey of juniper and its liquid derivatives is a long and illustrious one, with its story flowing from Greece to the Netherlands and Belgium to Britain before reaching America and swinging its way back into Europe and eventually reaching out into the rest of the world.

Gin in its modern form was first enjoyed in Belgium and the Netherlands – the gin we enjoy today is the evolution of a drink that began life as a spirit known as Jenever.

Juniper – or *jeneverbes* in Dutch – is a common species of evergreen plant – which grows prolifically across the mountains and heathlands of much of the northern hemisphere and Europe. The plants range from small bush-like shrubs up to towering trees, but it's the berry-like female seed cones that have been noted for millennia for their medicinal properties. From these tinctures and remedies, an appreciation of juniper's distinctively fruity, peppery flavour grew.

From the 1600s onwards, the trading power of the Dutch East India Trading Company meant that juniper outgrew its popularity in the Low Countries and went on to be transported around the world, eventually finding its way to England. There it fast became a favourite of soldiers – who, if you believe the stories, dubbed it 'Dutch Courage' after witnessing its nerve-calming and bravado-boosting properties in wars overseas. And, likewise, the nobility took to gin with relish, but with a slightly different agenda – they wished to ingratiate themselves with their newly crowned Dutch-born King William of Orange. Enjoyed by both the toughest and the most indulged members of late seventeenth-century society, cheap, easily produced imitations flooded the streets of London, leading to the creation of the spirit we now call gin.

In the first half of the eighteenth century – during what became known as the Gin Craze, a period when the juniper spirit spread like wildfire through the city of London – gin was outrageously, and some would say dangerously, popular in England. So much so that William Hogarth immortalised its perils in his 'Gin Lane' print as part of a propaganda campaign that led to the Gin Act of 1751. But while London was awash with gin, it never quite captured the imagination or drinking habits of the majority of Scots in the same way.

However, Jenever, as a distinct drink in its own right, remained a significant import into Edinburgh, through the port at Leith – huge quantities of which were also illegally smuggled into places like the fishing harbour along the shore at Newhaven – thanks to Scotland's trading links with the Low Countries. The tipple soon caught the attention of several notable Scottish figures, such as members of that famous distilling clan the Haigs, and they too dipped their toes into the production of a spirit so very different from our long established national drink. But outside of the capital's walls, *uisge beatha* – whisky – continued to reign supreme.

Nowadays, considering the vigour with which gin is produced north of the border, you'd be forgiven for thinking that it's a historic Scottish drink. This isn't quite the case, but Scotland has been tied to this wonderful tipple for a very long time, thanks to our nation's rich history of distillation, trade and, of course, innovation. In the past few centuries, many of the spices and herbs used in gin production were brought to Scottish shores via ports such as Leith, Dundee and Glasgow. At the same time, juniper, which was in plentiful supply in the north-eastern Highlands, was exported to the Netherlands to make Jenever.

However, it's only in the past two decades that gin's popularity has soared in Scotland. In the 1990s, the Scottish company United Distillers & Vintners – the forerunners of Diageo, the world's largest producer of spirits – made the decision to concentrate all their UK spirit production in Scotland. This was a game-changer: gin distillation once again took off in Scotland. In time, this would lead to nearly 70 per cent of the UK's gin being created in Scotland.

The 'small-batch gin wave' – that is, gin's answer to the craft beer movement – began after some quiet experiments by two distillers at whisky company Grant's. The team – master distiller David Stewart, and Hendrick's head distiller Lesley Gracie – wanted to create a premium alternative to that most famous of gin categories, London Dry. The pair were inspired by the successful launch of Bombay Sapphire in 1987, which gin expert Geraldine Coates believes was the true forerunner of a new premium gin sector. The 'lighter style' and striking blue bottle helped to 'revamp the image of the whole category, making it cool and sophisticated'.

Stewart and Gracie hoped to appeal to the modern consumer seeking authenticity and quality in a spirit. The result of their collaboration was Hendrick's. This gin was something of a slow burner: it launched in 2000 in the US and 2003 in the UK, but it was over a decade before it was recognised as a landmark, pioneering brand. With its kitsch Victoriana marketing, wonderfully accessible taste – and value-for-money price point – and that intriguing cucumber garnish, people slowly woke up to the idea that gin, which had been modestly holding its own in the vodka-dominated spirits market, could be cool again. Such a novel idea wasn't lost on a generation of drinkers who had grown tired of mass-produced alcohol brands and who were drawn to craft and provenance in everything from beer to bicycles. Indeed, the craft-beer market, and its surging popularity both here and in the States, helped to kickstart the growth of the craft spirits market.

Unsurprisingly, it was the whisky industry that first realised the potential of this new market in Scotland. Two of Scotland's expert whisky distillers, Inver House Distillers' Balmenach distiller Simon Buley and Bruichladdich's then master-distiller Jim McEwan, began to experiment with white spirits, soon launching the Caorunn and Botanist gins in 2009 and 2011 respectively. Other fledgling producers followed suit and the craft-gin industry was born.

Gin is relatively easy to produce in small quantities. And, as the revival of the juniper spirit took hold, the idea of not only drinking, but also *creating* gin didn't seem so very outlandish. More and more people began to experiment with the spirit, buying stills and creating their own new gins. Meanwhile, younger whisky companies, established on the basis of the phenomenal popularity of Scottish whisky, started to explore the possibility of using gin as a makeweight while they waited three years for their first whisky to mature in its casks.

This brings us to 2018, and the explosion of gin that's sending waves up and down the country. With new distilleries and companies opening all the time and domestic sales in the UK of £1.2 billion in the twelve months before September 2017 (that's the equivalent of 47 million bottles of gin!), now's the perfect time to raise a glass to this heady drink, and toast its renaissance in modern Scotland.

Gin Style

WHEN YOU ORDER a G&T – or something a little more adventurous – at your favourite local, the range of gins you'll be offered is greater now than ever before.

Even so, all gins must fit within certain parameters. Gin itself is legally defined as a spirit made from neutral spirit of agricultural origin – e.g. the potato and grain beloved of Slavic vodka – and flavoured with juniper berries. European Union regulations state that gin must be bottled with an alcoholic strength of no less than 37.5% ABV – it remains to be seen what will happen to British gin after Brexit – while in the United States it must be bottled at no less than 80° proof (40% ABV).

Creating gin requires artistry, patience and a lot of skill. From gin to genever, these are some of the most popular styles of gin you can enjoy when you order that G&T.

London Dry Gins

London Dry Gin is the classic juniper spirit and the best-known style of gin around the world today. The style was developed in the latter half of the eighteenth century, and, as most of its producers were based in London, it became known by the highly original moniker 'London Dry Gin'. However, despite its name, London Dry Gin does not need to be made in London – or even in the UK. The name now refers to any gin products produced under a set of strict EU regulations. These regulations dictate that the base spirit must be a completely neutral spirit, made purely from agricultural sources – meaning it cannot contain any artificial ingredients. After distillation, water and a minute quantity of sweetener can be added, but no additional flavours or colour.

Many distilleries have stayed true to the juniper-led flavour profile of London Dry Gin in their products – Tanqueray and Gordon's to name two of the most famous – but other producers – like St Andrews-based Eden Mill – are more experimental, using the time-honoured London Dry method to produce more unconventional gins with flavours that depart from the traditional.

Compound Gins

This style of gin differs from London Dry and other distilled gins in that flavours and botanicals can be added to the neutral spirit without re-distillation. This is sometimes referred to as the 'bathtub method', a term that comes from prohibition-era America, when people would make their own compound gin at home – usually in their bathtubs. In Scotland, Gin Bothy and Orkney are two of the best-known producers of compound gins.

Modern Gins

Modern, or contemporary, gins – which include Hendrick's – have a flavour that is not juniper-led. Juniper is present, but it does not dominate the flavour profile; instead, emphasis is placed more on the other botanicals used – herbal, floral or spicy. This type of gin is becoming more and more popular in the current gin revival.

Navy Strength Gins

The Navy has played an important role in gin's popularity, both in the UK and across the world. Sailors have long had a taste for the drink, and many of the earliest distilleries popped up in maritime cities, with gin being transported all over the world on naval ships.

Navy Strength Gin doesn't have a typical flavour profile that all producers adhere to; rather, gins in this category are united by their high alcohol content. Most have an ABV of 57%, or 100° UK proof. Historically, British naval soldiers tested a gin's strength by pouring it over gunpowder and then trying to light it. If it failed to light or fizzled, they knew the gin was diluted – and therefore unacceptable.

Many Scottish distilleries, such as North Berwick-based NB Gin, produce Navy Strength versions of their classic gin.

Genever

Dutch Genever, a predecessor to London Dry Gin, is made up of a blend of malt wine and neutral spirit. There are two types of this traditional juniper-flavoured spirit: *oude* (old) and *jonge* (young). However, these labels have nothing to do with age, and everything to do with the percentage of malt wine they contain. Oude Genever must have a malt-wine percentage of at least 15% – giving it a malty taste comparable with whisky – while Jonge Genever must have a percentage of no more than 15%. Juniper is the dominant flavour in both, and the inclusion of sugar adds richness to the taste.

Old Tom Gins

Old Tom Gin was popular in eighteenth-century England, a time when distilling practices were far from advanced. Gin was crude, unpalatable – and often dangerous. To mask its poor quality, producers laced it with the sweetest ingredients they could get their hands on, including sugar and liquorice. As a result, Old Tom Gin is often described as the bridge between Genever and Gin – sweeter than London Dry, but drier than Genever. It has more stories alluding to the origins of its name than The Botanist Gin has botanicals – and all fall at different places on the spectrum between the sublime and the ridiculous.

Flavoured gin liqueurs

These are usually lower in ABV than traditional gins, and tend to be far sweeter and more palatable than regular gins. Brands like Edinburgh Gin have taken advantage of the growing popularity of this gin style, producing a variety of fruity and floral flavoured liqueurs. Sloe Gin also belongs in this category.

Oak, cask and barrel-aged gins

These are gins that have been produced and then laid down in casks – mostly ex-whisky in Scotland – to 'mature', for anything from six weeks to ten months. This might sound a little strange. After all, gin is not a spirit associated with barrel ageing. However, it's not a new phenomenon; in the eighteenth and nineteenth centuries, oak was often used to store the spirit, rather than more easily breakable containers. Many producers swear by the process, arguing that barrel ageing imbues the gin with the classic spirit flavours that gin doesn't often contain, especially if the barrel has been used to age another spirit, like whisky, beforehand. As a result, barrel-aged gins often taste woody or smoky, and include notes of vanilla or caramel. Glasgow distillery Makar produces an oak-aged gin – a variant of their original gin.

Garnishes

FOR ALL THE gins in *Gin Galore*, you'll find garnish suggestions for each one; these are chosen by the gin producers themselves. A good garnish is the perfect accompaniment to a gin-based drink: it will appeal to the eyes, tease with its aroma, and give depth to the drink's taste, accentuating the gin's unique flavour.

These recommended combinations are designed to be a steady, tried and tested ground from which to branch out and experiment with different ingredients and flavours. The beauty of this spirit is that it is one of the most versatile, so if you don't like a particular garnish, don't be afraid to switch it out for something you prefer. After all, it's you who will be drinking it (along with your friends, of course) so try out anything you like – it's part of the fun!

The same goes for mixers. Many people assume they don't like gin because they don't like tonic. But while gin and tonic are old pals, they aren't exclusive – other mixers like lemonade, soda and ginger ale make excellent date-mates too.

What is the function of a garnish? Essentially, it's an additive that either complements and accentuates a gin's key flavours, or contrasts and clashes with them. The result is a harmonious balance in flavour, or an unusual combination that will excite and challenge the taste buds.

A Glossary of Garnishes

Here are some of the terms you will see used in this book and what they mean.

Slice Fairly self-explanatory: a finely cut piece of fruit.

Wedge A thicker segment or slice of fruit.

Twist and peel A thin slice of the peel of a citrus fruit. Cut using a peeler, with the pith (the fruit's spongy inner lining) carefully removed to avoid added bitterness.

In mixology, the term 'twist' refers to the act of squeezing the oils from the peel by twisting it over the drink before garnishing.

Expert's tip: to add a visual flourish to your drink, wrap a thin strip of the peel round a paper straw to give it shape, then hang it over the edge of the glass.

Sprigs or leaves An individual leaf or strand of a particular herb or plant.

Grated Using a fine grater, grate a small amount of the chosen spice into the drink.

The Beauty of Botanicals

TRADITIONALLY DESCRIBED AS 'any substance derived from parts of a plant and used in making medicine', the word botanical has taken on a new life of its own within the drinks industry. Now synonymous with gin, it usually refers to the herbs, seeds, roots, berries, and fruits that help to flavour the spirit used to create gin.

Each of these botanicals are selected and combined – in much the same way as a recipe – to create a delicate symphony of flavour that will create the character of the final spirit. However, the juniper berries must contribute the predominant flavour if the drink is to be classed as gin. From there on, anything goes when it comes to which additional botanicals are included.

Jamie Shields, of the Summerhall Drinks Lab in Edinburgh, likens the process to making a curry; each person will have their own idea of what constitutes the best recipe – an opinion at least partly driven by the idiosyncrasies of their own taste buds – despite many curries sharing the same three or four defining base ingredients.

And that is the magic of gin, too. Each recipe can be tailored to an individual's preferred tastes and adapted to include ingredients specific to the region in which the gin is made. Perhaps, in time, this will give rise to the gin category gaining its own form of terroir – like Champagne.

In Scotland, it's this sense of provenance and regionality, rather than the mere attachment of a place name to a product, that gives producers their ability to create point of difference in a crowded and competitive market.

And so here is a guide to some of the more prominent botanicals, from the five main traditional options through to some of the more innovative ones used by Scottish gin producers.

Five traditional botanicals

Juniper berries

These are to gin what grapes are to wine and malted barley is to single-malt whisky. They are the key ingredient that makes gin, gin. Juniper is responsible for that wonderful pine-forest aroma and flavour that makes this spirit so enticing.

Traditionally, juniper was abundant in Scotland. Now, the plants struggle to mature because the country's deer population like to eat them. Most producers now source the berries from places such as Italy, Macedonia, Bulgaria and even Croatia.

Coriander seeds

Sourced in southern Europe, Morocco and India, coriander seeds – not the divisive plant – are often described as the second most important botanical in gin-making. These small yellow seeds link particularly well with juniper berries, adding citrus notes and a little spice to the final spirit.

Angelica root

Native to countries in the northern hemisphere, angelica is found throughout Europe. The roots – and occasionally seeds – are used in gin-making to provide a base earthiness. They also help to bond many of the other flavours together.

Orris root

The root of the iris flower is used in many gins, although the high cost of the powder – a consequence of its labour-intensive processing – means it is used sparingly.

The root is highly prized in the perfume-making industry, thanks to its ability to bond and enhance other – usually lighter – aromas. It's useful to gin distillers for the same reason. Not entirely aroma-free, orris provides a light, sweet floral note said to be akin to the old-school British sweet – the Parma violet.

Citrus

Citrus provides that clean, refreshing top note in a gin. This sweet, zesty flavour is usually provided by lemon and orange peel – although sometimes the fruit is used in its entirety. In recent times, a wider variety of citrus fruits has started appearing in recipe lists. Limes, blood oranges, grapefruits and yuzu offer more unusual flavour notes.

Other traditional botanicals

Liquorice root

Used mainly as a sweetening agent, liquorice also provides light notes of aniseed.

Aniseed, star anise and fennel seeds

Much like liquorice root, these provide different variations of that earthy aniseed flavour.

Cassia bark and cinnamon

These two spices are very similar and stem from a common family tree – in fact, cassia is often mis-sold as cinnamon. They both provide a warm, woody spiciness to gin.

Green cardamom seeds

Unmistakably perfumed, these provide a sweet, warming note, with a fresh hint of eucalyptus.

Common Scottish botanicals

Sea buckthorn berries

Commonly found around Scotland's coasts, this aromatic plant's berries are quite tart and provide a fresh, fruity top note.

Rowan berries

Abundant in Scotland's forests and woodlands, rowan berries have a delicate flavour, which provides a sweet, slightly bitter-tasting note.

Bog myrtle

A common sight in Scotland, these industrious little shrubs have been used in everything from medicine-making to brewing, and are well known as a great midge repellent. They offer a baseline of resinous notes such as wood and pine.

Heather

A plant common throughout Scotland, heather provides a grassy, floral note with hints of honey.

Gorse

Not heavily used in gin-making, gorse, very common throughout the UK, is said to produce a coconut-like scent when picked.

Bladderwrack seaweed

This distinctive and nutritious seaweed can be found on coastlines around the UK and provides a salty tasting note, which can riff off the more traditional base botanicals.

Nettles

Another common garden weed that has been given a new lease of life as an ingredient in gin-making, nettles have been used in brewing and cooking for centuries and provide a fresh, grassy flavour.

Rosehips

Better known by Scots of a certain age as 'itchy coos', rosehips are the deep orangey-red fruit of the wild rose. They provide a lovely floral sweetness.

The Gins

Achroous Gin

Electric Spirit Co., Tower Street Stillhouse, Leith, Edinburgh EH6 7BX
www.facebook.com/electricspiritco
Price £37 / *Quantity* 700ml / *ABV* 41%

THE GROWTH OF distilling in Scotland's capital has been forging ahead with quite some vigour in recent years, with brands such as Edinburgh Gin and Pickering's pushing the juniper spirit's renaissance, and with new whisky distilleries being announced in the Southside and Leith. It's in the latter area of the city that we find one of Edinburgh's most exciting up-and-coming gin producers.

A one-man show, the Electric Spirit Co., which is now based at Tower Street, was founded by MSc-educated distiller James Porteous at the end of 2014, with the brand's original micro-distillery in Leith following in 2015.

The rich history of the port of Leith can be traced back to 1544. From the 1770s onwards it flourished to become one of the most important docks, trade hubs and industrial centres of Victorian times. It's long had a connection to both the trade of gin and its creation, and re-establishing those historic links lies at the heart of what Porteous and the ESC aim to do.

The idea for the gin's branding began with some scribbles based on a simplified image of a light bulb. Porteous says this represents the innovative, entrepreneurial ideas that are the brand's distinctive hallmark, adding that he chose the electric name to reflect the thoughts around the vivid designs and flavours that are the founding principles of his company.

The spirit of partnership that has become so prevalent in the drinks industry is another element that the ESC founder is keen to develop, leading him to create gin collaborations with events like North Hop and the Gin Festival, and Edinburgh drinks company Solid Liquids. The ESC's relationship with Edinburgh's Timberyard restaurant has seen the creation of a series of single-botanical distillates using gorse flower, lemon verbena and Scots pine, all distilled on a rotary evaporator.

Having recently expanded its capacity, the Leith-based company has created a lasting partnership with the newly founded Port of Leith Distillery. It's also looking to take its gin beyond Scotland while experimenting with new ideas and recipes.

Achroous Gin

The first thing you'll notice about Achroous Gin is the striking neon orange bottle, a branding that seems a touch ironic given that the name of the gin springs from the ancient Greek word for colourless or achromatic. However, Porteous is quick to explain that this refers to the gin and not the bottle.

To make the Achroous, the Leith-based distiller uses juniper and coriander as well as other traditional ingredients such as orris, liquorice and angelica root, alongside two more unusual botanicals in the form of fennel seed and Szechuan peppercorn. Where the former provides a 'lovely anise sweetness', the latter adds a 'woody, floral aroma' and an 'almost sherbet citrus on the tongue'.

Each of these botanicals has, according to the young distiller, been chosen to create a tangible impact on the character of the finished spirit, with nothing there simply for 'the sake of marketing'.

Preferred serve

A double over lots of good ice, with Fever-Tree Naturally Light Tonic to taste – it's a bit less sugary than other tonics and gives a much drier drink.

Preferred garnish

Though not a fan of garnishing a G&T, Porteous says a slice of lemon or grapefruit works well with the spirit if you're keen to add some fruit.

Botanicals

Juniper, coriander, orris, liquorice, angelica, fennel seed and
Szechuan peppercorns.

Recommended cocktail

Negroni

The producer says, 'I love the way it makes a negroni taste. You need
bold flavours to avoid getting lost in a glass with Campari and the
vermouth, but I think a good whack of juniper and the character of the
fennel seed and peppercorns really shines through.'

Ingredients
25ml Achroous Gin
25ml vermouth rosso
25ml Campari
1 orange twist

Method

Pour the gin, vermouth rosso and Campari into a glass, mix well, then
strain into a glass with ice. Garnish with a twist of orange peel.

Edinburgh Gin

Edinburgh Gin Distillery and Visitor Centre, 1A Rutland Place,
Edinburgh EH1 2AD *and* The Biscuit Factory Distillery,
4–6 Anderson Place, Leith, Edinburgh EH6 5NP
www.edinburghgin.com
Price £29.95 / *Quantity* 700ml / *ABV* 43%

THE CAPITAL IS as rich in its heritage of distilling and brewing as it is in history and architecture, so it might come as a surprise to learn that until Pickering's opened their distillery at Summerhall in 2014, there hadn't been a distillery exclusively producing gin in the city for nearly one hundred and fifty years.

Surprising because, in the late eighteenth century, there were no less than eight licensed stills in Edinburgh. Perhaps even more incredibly, the legal operations were far outnumbered by the illicit stills at the time with the number suspected to be around four hundred or so. That's before you factor in that Leith was once a centre of trade for many types of spirit, including genever – gin's Dutch predecessor.

What's more, in 2018, it's claimed that the Scottish capital's residents are drinking more gin per head than any other British city. And it's this demand for gin that has been successfully met by the launch of Edinburgh Gin, arguably one of the most successful Scottish brands outwith the big three – Caorunn, the Botanist and Hendrick's.

Founded by drinks industry veterans Alex and Jane Nicol in 2010, the fledgling brand took on distiller and graduate of Heriot-Watt's Brewing and Distilling course David Wilkinson in 2014 as part of a Knowledge Transfer Partnership with the university. Then, in summer 2014, Edinburgh Gin made its home in the basement below the Rutland Hotel as it opened the new distillery and in-house gin bar Heads and Tales, where Flora and Caledonia – the brand's stills – are housed.

Launched with its classic gin, Edinburgh Gin quickly followed up with the release of the Cannonball Gin, named for the city's rich naval heritage and the famous One o'Clock Gun. This 'navy-strength' gin comes in at 100% proof (57.2% ABV) and features twice the juniper content of the classic Edinburgh Gin, with Szechuan peppercorns added to the recipe to create a spicy kick.

In May 2016, the popularity of Edinburgh Gin led to the opening of a second distillery in an arts and fashion hub in what was once the old Crawford's biscuit factory in Leith. This second unit has the capacity to produce enough gin to create about 2.5 million G&Ts a year.

The producer's fruit gin liqueurs have also become hugely popular since their launch, with flavours including rhubarb and ginger, plum and vanilla, elderflower and raspberry. Bottled at 20% ABV, this fun range combines Edinburgh Gin with fruits that have been previously macerated in pure sugar cane.

The brand's core gin range includes their Seaside Gin, Cannonball Gin and Edinburgh Gin 1670.

Edinburgh Gin

Described as a 'classic London Dry-style gin', this was the first expression to be released by the Nicols in 2010 when they created the Edinburgh Gin brand.

Created by hand in small batches at both the West End and Leith distilleries, Edinburgh Gin is made using a blend of fourteen botanicals, including lavender, pine buds, mulberries and cobnuts. In designing a gin that tastes clean, zesty and juniper-forward, the EG team also used orange peel, lemongrass and lime peel to create fresh, uplifting citrus notes.

Preferred serve

Serve in a tall glass with ice, using equal parts gin and good quality tonic water, with an orange peel to garnish.

Preferred garnish

A twist of orange peel.

Botanicals

Juniper, orange peel, mulberries, pine buds, lavender, lemongrass, milk thistle, coriander, cobnuts, lime peel, orange peel and orris root.

Recommended cocktail

The Edinburgh Gin Gimlet

Ingredients
50ml Edinburgh Gin
5ml fresh lime juice
5ml Rose's Lime Cordial
Lime twist

Method

Shake the ingredients together with ice. Strain into a coupe glass and garnish with a lime twist.

Pickering's

Pickering's Gin Distillery, 1 Summerhall, Summerhall Distillery,
Edinburgh EH9 1PL
www.pickeringsgin.com
Price £29.95 / *Quantity* 700ml / *ABV* 42%

THE GERM OF the idea that would go on to form Pickering's Gin first formulated in 2012 when Matthew Gammell and Marcus Pickering took possession of a handwritten scrap of paper, which dated back to 17 July 1947. Given to them by a friend of Pickering's father, it detailed a traditional Bombay gin recipe made using nine botanicals.

Based at Summerhall and having witnessed the successful launch of a brewery on the site, Pickering and Gammell decided to create a gin distillery on the part of the complex that formerly housed the dog kennels of the old Royal (Dick) School of Veterinary Studies, and perfect a re-creation of their Bombay recipe.

In 2014 everything was ready and – after numerous trials to perfect their gin – a modern version of the original recipe was born. Named Pickering's after its founder, the flagship gin was soon followed by two more expressions, each marked out by the colours of their wax tops – red, orange and black.

The first, the Navy Strength, was created in 2014 in celebration of the brand becoming the official gin sponsor of the Royal Edinburgh Military Tattoo, while the second, the Original 1947, was made to the original recipe gifted to the pair on that scrap of paper.

The brand went on to create one of their most popular products in the winter of 2014 – with their award-winning gin baubles gaining notoriety as far away as the United States; the final December 2016 batch was a record-breaker with a run of 30,000 selling out in just 82 seconds.

Sold in packs of six, the colourful baubles each contain a 50ml serving of Pickering's signature gin; over a million of the drinks-themed Christmas ornaments have now been sold.

Pickering's Gin

Pickering's premium gin is made using nine distinct botanicals with fennel, anise, lemon, lime and cloves added to the traditional stalwarts of juniper, coriander, cardamom and angelica. The angelica was used a substitute for the cinnamon to create a modern version of the original recipe that Matt inherited.

Described as 'a spectacularly smooth and flavoursome London dry-style gin', Pickering's is produced in Gertrude and Emily – the two 500-litre gin stills named after the founders' grandmothers – that feature a slow heating process which means Matt and the team can control the temperature to within one degree of accuracy.

Each and every bottle of gin produced at the distillery is then labelled, corked and dipped in wax by hand before shipping; the distillery team say that this process of hand-finishing is still hugely important to them.

Preferred serve

In a glass with ice, tonic and a slice of pink grapefruit.

Preferred garnish

Pink grapefruit.

Botanicals

Fennel, anise, lemon, lime peel, cloves, juniper, coriander, cardamom and angelica.

Recommended cocktail

The Lavender Negroni

Ingredients
25ml Pickering's Gin
25ml Campari
25ml lavender vermouth

Method
Add everything to an ice-filled rocks glass and stir gently for 45 to 60 seconds. Garnish with a pink grapefruit twist.

Note
To create your own lavender-infused vermouth, mix dried lavender with bianco vermouth at a ratio of 10 to 1 vermouth to flowers. Leave it to macerate for at least forty-eight hours then strain out the flowers.

4 Apothecary Rose Gin

The Old Curiosity Distillery, 32A Old Pentland Road,
Edinburgh EH10 7EA
www.theoldcuriosity.co.uk
Price £35.95 / *Quantity* 500ml / *ABV* 39%

FEW DISTILLERS CAN claim to have the botanical pedigree of renowned Scottish herbologist Hamish Martin, who founded and runs Edinburgh's Secret Herb Garden.

Nestled at the foot of the Pentland Hills close to the capital, the herb nursery was opened in 2014 when Hamish sold his wine business and set about fulfilling his dream with his wife Liberty, moving their family, five dogs and a cat into a static caravan and building their garden from the ground up.

Now hugely successful, the garden is home to seven and a half acres of land with five hundred types of herbs, a bee conservatory, a café, a shop and, launched in February 2018, a gin distillery.

Founded by Hamish, it took almost a year to convert one of the garden's barns into a still room, before he and head distiller Mark Boswell set about creating a core range of floral gins – with Apothecary Rose, Lavender & Echinacea and Chamomile & Cornflower being the first three releases.

Each of the gins is infused with apothecary plants that are grown and handpicked in the Secret Herb Garden – and they are all 100 per cent natural, and free of any sugar or chemicals.

In June 2018, the team followed up their gin launch with a UK first – a gin garden where visitors can observe the selection and picking of the botanicals, the drying process, right through to the distilling. The garden is packed with 1,500 juniper bushes – which will take a few years to be ready – complemented by eighty herbs and floral varieties such as scented lemon verbena, geraniums, irises and roses.

The opening of the gin garden coincided with the launch of two new seasonal, limited edition gins. Bringing to life a selection of summery flavours, the Old Curiosity's Geranium & Mallow and Damask Rose were available in limited batches of just five hundred.

Apothecary Rose Gin

The true magic of this gin is not just its flavour but the fact that when you add tonic to the golden spirit, it changes colour to a light pink.

The Apothecary Rose that gives the gin its name is aptly titled. As one of the oldest rose varieties in the world, it has been used in tinctures and tonics for centuries – and for this gin it is only harvested for three weeks a year, from the gin garden itself.

Subtle in fragrance, elegant and 'naturally floral in flavour', it's a playful gin that works with a variety of mixers but perhaps best with a light tonic.

Preferred serve

Use a light Fever-Tree Indian Tonic Water, add plenty of ice to a balloon glass and garnish with some rose petals.

Preferred garnish

Rose petals.

Botanicals

Juniper, coriander, winter savoury, angelica and Apothecary Rose.

Ispahan Club

Created by Jamie Shields of Summerhall Drinks Lab.

Ingredients
40ml Apothecary Rose Gin
10ml lychee liqueur
10ml sweet vermouth
20ml lemon juice
15ml raspberry syrup
2 dashes of vegan foamer, or
1 egg white
Candied rose petals to garnish

Method
Dry shake all the ingredients together with no ice, add ice and shake again. Double-strain into a champagne coupe and garnish with candied rose petals.

For the raspberry syrup
Simmer 500ml of boiling water with 1kg of sugar and stir until dissolved. Take off the heat and add 250g of raspberries. Mash raspberries and allow one to two hours to infuse. Strain through muslin and squeeze out any excess liquid and pour into a sterilised glass bottle. Your syrup will last in the fridge for a month, or add a dash of vodka to extend its shelf life to six months.

NB Gin

NB Distillery Limited, Halflandbarns, North Berwick EH39 5PW
www.nbdistillery.com
Price £25 / *Quantity* 700ml / *ABV* 42%

ALONG THE COAST from the capital, on the shoreline of Scotland's outstanding golf coast, lies the seaside town of North Berwick, and the home of one of the country's most successful gins.

Founded in 2013 by husband and wife partnership, Steve and Vivienne Muir, the NB Gin team moved into a new distillery and luxury visitor attraction in 2018, reflecting the success the brand has had since its formation. Their gin is now exported across the Atlantic to the United States.

This reach is a far cry from their origins as a 'kitchen ginnery' with Viv and Steve experimenting in their home with a 'pressure cooker and some old central heating pipes' to create a range of recipes in their pursuit of what they describe as the perfect London style gin.

Distilled using only eight botanicals – Viv claims they only need those eight to create a classic gin – NB won a silver medal at the Gin Masters awards at the first time of asking and, even more impressively, was voted the 'Best London Dry Gin' at the World Drinks Awards in 2015.

NB are regular sponsors of the BRIT Awards after-party, but it's not just music royalty who've noticed the quality of their gin. Indeed, the Queen chose NB as the only gin brand to appear in her official commemorative publication for her ninetieth birthday celebrations.

NB Gin now comes in two editions: the classic London Dry, and NB Navy Strength London Dry, a navy-strength gin at 57% ABV. Recently, what is described as the 'world's first London Dry citrus vodka' was also added to the NB core range.

The Muirs and their team designed their new distillery to be energy neutral, with solar panels providing much of the power and a special system built to capture rain water, store it and allow it to be reused for the condensing process of stilling. And now, situated at Halfland Barns, near the fourteenth-century Tantallon Castle, the 2018 opening of the NB visitor centre will bring fans closer to the gin than ever before with bespoke tours filled with sampling, learning, luxury and even canapés by award-winning local chef, John Paul McLachlan.

NB Gin

As a London Dry Gin, NB is a true traditional gin lover's gin with big hits of juniper followed by clean notes of citrus and a slight spice that adds a nice complexity.

Bottled at 42% ABV, it works as well neat over ice as it does with a mixer or as the base spirit in a cocktail. The Muirs have also teamed up with Bon Accord soft drinks to create their own tonic water designed as the perfect complement to NB gin and their spirits range.

Preferred serve

Serve with NB Tonic, over ice and garnish with a peel of orange or a slice of pink grapefruit.

Preferred garnish

Peel of orange or a slice of pink grapefruit.

Botanicals

Juniper, coriander seed, cassia bark, orris root, cardamom, lemon peel and grains of paradise.

B's Knees

This cocktail was created especially for the BRIT Awards.

Ingredients
50ml NB Gin
25ml lemon juice
25ml B's syrup

For the B's syrup
250ml bees' honey
125ml hot water
2 rosemary sprigs
5g crushed black peppercorns

Method
First create the syrup mix by mixing the syrup ingredients together and allowing them to cool. Then add all of the gin, lemon juice and syrup to a shaker and shake over ice before double-straining into a coupe glass. No garnish required.

Makar

The Glasgow Distillery Company, Hillington,
Deanside Road, Glasgow G52 4XB
www.glasgowdistillery.com
Price £35 / *Quantity* 700ml / *ABV* 43%

SCOTLAND'S BIGGEST CITY is home to the Glasgow Distillery, a production site that can be found in the Southside at Hillington Park. It recently not only produced its awarding-winning gin Makar, but is also Glasgow's first independent single malt whisky distillery since 1902.

Named after the ancient Scots word for 'the maker or craftsman', the distilling team say their flagship gin's moniker reflects the creativity and craft that's invested so carefully in its production. This unassuming distillery hidden away in an industrial estate in Hillington really is a spirits marvel. It might be small, but it produces no fewer than four styles of gin, one vodka and a single malt whisky – with many more set to follow.

Established in 2013 by drinks industry veterans Liam Hughes, Mike Hayward and Ian McDougall, the Glasgow Distillery Company saw their distillery built just one year later in 2014, with each of the site's three German-made stills named after close members of the three founders' families.

Two were named Tara and Mhairi after Liam's daughter and Ian's daughter respectively, while the third Annie – named for Mike's great-grandmother, who introduced him to gin and instilled in him a passion for making the juniper-led spirit – is used to create their distinctive gin.

Forward-thinking and innovative, the Glasgow Distillery Company have a young distilling team, half of which are female, with a keen focus on the Glasgow community leading to key partnerships with businesses such as Glasgow airport. This synchronised outlook means that Makar gin is the first that many will meet on their arrival into the city.

Makar

When it was first released in 2014, Makar marked another first for the company: it became the first gin to be distilled in Glasgow.

Its distinctive tall bottle immediately draws the eye and, of course, there's symbolism in its design with each of the seven sides representing one of the seven carefully selected botanicals chosen to combine with juniper to create a traditional, juniper-forward gin.

Angelica, liquorice, black peppercorns and cassia bark are combined with juniper berries in the pot of Annie – the copper still – before the lemon, coriander and rosemary are vapour infused in the helmet to create a gin whose heavy rosemary overtures give it a big vibrant flavour that really stands out from the crowd.

Preferred serve

In a glass with ice, a high-quality tonic water and a slice of mild green chilli as a garnish.

Preferred garnish

Mild green chilli.

Botanicals

Coriander, angelica, lemon, liquorice, black peppercorns, cassia bark and rosemary.

Dry Makar Martini

Ingredients
50ml Makar Gin
15ml dry vermouth
A dash of orange bitters
A twist of orange or lemon peel to garnish

Method
Pour the Makar, vermouth and orange bitters into a glass and stir
for twenty to thirty seconds, then strain into a classic cocktail glass
and add the twist of orange or lemon peel to garnish.

Crossbill

Crossbill Highland Distilling, The Hatchery, BAaD,
Calton Entry, Glasgow G40 2SB
www.crossbillgin.com
Price £38 / *Quantity* 750ml / *ABV* 43.8%

NAMED AFTER THE UK's only endemic bird species, the Scottish Crossbill, this thrilling brand brings a little bit of the Highlands to the east end of Glasgow.

Aberdeenshire native Jonathan Engels created his own brand of gin terroir when he became the first Scottish producer to revert to the tradition of using wild Scottish juniper to make gin, reflecting a time when the country's juniper stocks were exported to the Netherlands to make genever.

Beginning his journey in the Inshriach Estate – where he built his own distillery in what would go on to become UK Shed of the Year in 2015 – Jonathan enlisted the help of volunteers to cultivate the wild berries found on the estate to create his small-batch gin.

In 2017 Engels moved his operation to Glasgow. This meant he could increase production to match demand for his popular gin as well as founding the Crossbill gin school, something he had always been keen to do.

The Crossbill founder now regularly invites locals and guests alike to the distillery at the Hatchery, Glasgow, where they can enjoy a tutored tasting and use their own choice of botanicals in miniature copper stills to create uniquely individual gins.

The gin producer has also since formed an alliance with the Forestry Commission and PlantLife.org and now picks his juniper from other estates in the Highlands.

Harvested in small amounts, and only when they are three years old, the distiller explains that this helps to ensure the sustainability of the wild crops, with each batch reflecting the ancient highland juniper forests from where they were picked.

To highlight this, the distiller created the small-batch Crossbill 200, which features juniper sourced only from a single 200-year-old tree.

The pioneering gin brand has also added a limited edition pineapple gin liqueur and a sumac gin to their range. This exciting expression is created using staghorn sumac, a botanical found in New Hampshire, the natural habitat of the Scottish Crossbill's cousin, the North American Red Crossbill.

Crossbill Gin

Described as a celebration of juniper and rosehip, two 'bold and fresh Highland botanicals', Crossbill is made in small batches and aims to reflect the terroir of the Scottish juniper. Unusually, it only uses these two botanicals, distilled in a ratio of 60:40 to ensure the juniper takes the lead when it comes to the final spirit.

Crossbill is a real 'gin lover's gin' in which the refreshing pine-y notes of the juniper give way to a delicious hit of citrus – perfect for those who appreciate that traditional style.

Preferred serve

Serve in a glass with ice and one part gin to two parts Fever-Tree and garnish with a twist of orange.

Preferred garnish

A twist of orange.

Botanicals

Scottish juniper and rosehip.

Garden Martini

Ingredients
45ml Crossbill Gin
25ml Pincer Botanical Vodka
15ml lime juice
A dash of elderflower cordial
½ sprig of rosemary
5 basil leaves
2 lime wedges
A bay leaf to garnish

Method
Muddle the lime, basil and rosemary, then add the Pincer, Crossbill, elderflower cordial and lime juice, then shake and double-strain into a chilled martini glass. Garnish with a bay leaf.

eeNoo

The Lost Loch Distillery, Unit 7, Deeside Activity Park,
Dess, Aboyne AB34 5BD
www.lostlochdistillery.com
Price £37 / *Quantity* 700ml / *ABV* 43%

HEAD WEST FROM Aberdeen and follow the winding River Dee through the rolling hills and sprawling rural scenery of Royal Deeside, and you'll eventually come to one of the most whimsical spirits producers Scotland has to offer. Lost Loch Distillery was set up by Peter Dignan and Richard Pierce in 2017 and is named after Loch Auchlossan. The spirits producer can be found on the historic eastern shore of this 'lost' body of water.

Lovers of alcoholic drinks and their history, Dignan and Pierce's pioneering claim to fame is that they are the first distillery team in the country to have produced their own absinthe – Murmichan, which takes its wonderfully evocative title from the name of a wicked Scottish fairy.

Their small-batch gin, which followed shortly after Murmichan, is called eeNoo after the old Scots phrase meaning 'just now', 'at the present time', or 'at once'. Designed to be a traditional gin modelled on the juniper spirits of old, eeNoo also features a selection of botanicals sourced locally.

The spirits range, the majority of which is produced on a 500-litre still and a smaller traditional copper alembic still, now includes new addition Haroosh – a brambleberry and whisky liqueur. All of the production, bottling and labelling still takes place at their highland distillery.

In addition, the pair have gone to great lengths to source as much of their energy as they can from sustainable sources; a percentage of the power and heat used at the distillery comes from renewable sources such as a wind turbine, solar panel array and biomass boiler – all located on site.

eeNoo

The eeNoo recipe is filled with botanicals designed to evoke the Scottish Highlands at each taste. The most predominant of these is Royal Deeside honey, which has a flavour profile unique to the region with heather, willow herb and clover pollen all contributing to its distinctive make-up.

Heather flowers and soft fruits such as brambleberries and raspberries sourced from berry farms in Aberdeenshire, Deeside and Angus are the perfect complementary flavours.

This leads to a traditional juniper flavour coupled with notes of Scottish berries and a lingering spice. The result is then lovingly bottled by hand and given a striking label featuring artwork that references an enigmatic Inuit traveller named Eenoolooapik who, according to the distillers, visited Scotland, and in particular the city of Aberdeen, in the early nineteenth century.

Preferred serve

In a glass with ice, topped up with Lamb and Watt tonic and garnished with diced strawberries.

Preferred garnish

Diced strawberries.

Botanicals

Royal Deeside honey, heather flowers, brambleberries, raspberries, Italian juniper, rosehip, coriander seeds, angelica root, liquorice root, almonds, pepper, orange and lemon peel.

Recommended cocktail

The Lost Loch

Ingredients
50ml eeNoo
10ml Haroosh
2 dashes of Murmichan
30ml fresh orange juice

Method
Add all the ingredients to an ice-filled shaker and shake for a good twenty to thirty seconds. Strain into a tall glass.

Esker Gin

Esker Spirits Ltd, 1 Westhall Workshops,
Kincardine O'Neil, Aboyne AB34 5AE
www.eskerspirits.com
Price £37.50 / *Quantity* 700ml / *ABV* 42%

THE STUNNING SETTING of Royal Deeside, and the valley of the River Dee, is home to the summer residence of the royal family, Balmoral Castle, but also to a brilliant new gin producer.

Esker Gin is the brainchild of Stephen and Lynne Duthie, a couple who grew up in the North East and wanted to create a gin brand that would reflect the stunning vistas of their local surroundings. Having founded the distillery in October 2015, the pair went on to launch their first gin in June 2016, featuring an intriguing, locally sourced botanical unique in Scotland to Esker: silver birch sap.

Before that, the set-up began life as a series of experiments in a small still in their kitchen, which then emigrated to a shed in the garden before moving to the Kincardine Estate in 2017 – an upscale that was due both to increased demand for the gin and to gain easier access to their unique botanical.

Chosen for its curiously sweet flavour, the Duthies source the silver birch sap from the trees of the Kincardine Estate, which along with heather flowers and rosehip, provides the provenance the pair were keen to create when establishing the brand.

Determined to build a company they could be proud of, the Duthies have put people and sustainability at the heart of their operation, with anyone who works for Esker, be it full-time, part-time, temporary or ad-hoc event staff, paid significantly over the national living wage, regardless of age.

In addition, they were one of the first in the craft spirits industry to introduce a scheme where customers can return their empty bottle at events in return for a discount on their purchase. Their zero-waste policy means that effluent (waste product from stills) is now given to the estate's farmers to put on their fields to feed the earth.

The Duthies plan to expand on their drinks range beyond the two gins they currently have – the Esker and the Esker Honey Spiced Gin – because, as Stephen explains, the firm is called Esker Spirits, 'rather than just Esker Gin' meaning they have the potential to diversify their spirits portfolio.

Esker Gin

Designed to be a classic juniper-led gin but with hidden depth, Esker takes a little sweetness from its silver birch sap as well as floral notes from rosehip and heather. The recipe took over two years of experimentation to perfect with the Scottish botanicals added to traditional ingredients sourced elsewhere, such as pink peppercorns and cassia, to create a complex gin full of appeal to traditionalists.

The modern design of the bottle features references to the River Dee, the Deeside topography, the silver birch and, of course, a hint of tartan.

Preferred serve

Over ice with a good tonic and a twist of orange peel. However, the Esker team encourage people to experiment. The gin can also be taken neat over ice, or mixed with cloudy lemonade or a ginger ale, then garnished with pink grapefruit, cinnamon stick or rosemary.

Preferred garnish

A twist of orange peel.

Botanicals

Juniper, pink peppercorn, citrus, cassia, heather, rosehip, milk thistle and silver birch sap.

The Apple Charlotte

Ingredients
30ml Esker Gin
15ml vermouth
30ml pressed apple juice
30ml ginger beer
Crystallised (candied) ginger

Method
Mix all the ingredients in a tall glass over ice and garnish with the
crystallised (candied) ginger.

10

LoneWolf London Dry

LoneWolf Spirits, Balmacassie Industrial Estate,
Balmacassie Drive, Ellon AB41 8BX
www.lonewolfspirits.com
Price £32 / *Quantity* 700ml / *ABV* 44%

THESE DAYS THE North East has a lot to shout about when it comes to food and drink, not just that which is found on its farms and fishing boats, but also in terms of what its breweries and distilleries produce. Home to one of the country's – and arguably the world's – top craft beer producers as well as some world-class single-malt whisky distilleries, Aberdeenshire can now add gin to its long list of potable delights.

LoneWolf, the spirits company created by craft beer giants BrewDog in April 2017, is one of the only grain-to-glass distillers in the country. The team at Ellon controls every aspect of their gin's production. The brand's own vodka is made with a 50:50 blend of malted wheat and malted barley. It's created in the specially designed distilling equipment – which features an 18-metre high column – before the botanicals are added to create their signature London Dry Gin.

Much like their desire to create top-quality innovative craft beers, BrewDog and, in this instance, LoneWolf have embraced that love of non-conformity and applied it to their spirits. The team are keen to point out that although provenance is important, it isn't the overriding factor in creating quality gin. With that in mind, they have selected botanicals based on their ability to impart the best flavours and work harmoniously alongside one another to create a 'perfectly balanced flavour profile'.

The one botanical, of the fourteen they use, which is local to them are the needles of the Scots pine, a tree that grows in abundance in Aberdeenshire and imparts a unique flavour to their London Dry gin.

Alongside the London Dry, LoneWolf also produce a Navy Strength Gunpowder Gin, which they launched in 2017, as well as a barrel-aged single-malt character vodka – held in charred American oak for eleven months – and a cranachan vodka.

Never ones to hold back when it comes to the pursuit of bright, shiny things, the Lone Wolf team have even taken the hassle out of choosing a tonic by releasing a canned G&T that has the perfect ratio of LoneWolf London Dry and their own specially created tonic water.

LoneWolf London Dry

Described as 'purity personified' and a 'gin with bite', LoneWolf London Dry was created after a long series of experiments to formulate a perfectly balanced recipe designed to maximise flavour.

Featuring fourteen botanicals, LoneWolf begins with a body of citrus giving way to a delicate spiciness before the lavender provides a wonderfully floral finish. This is a gin with depth and complexity that rewards the drinker with its different qualities at every sip.

As would be expected from the spirits arm of BrewDog, the bottle packaging is deliberately minimalist with the removable label attached to the bottle by a thick black rubber band and the black wolf's head sitting proudly on both the bottle (under the label) and on the label itself.

Preferred serve

Serve over ice in a 1:3 ratio of LoneWolf Gin to LoneWolf Tonic.

Preferred garnish

A twist of pink grapefruit peel, pith removed.

Botanicals

Juniper, Scots pine, fresh grapefruit peel, fresh lemon peel, coriander seed, cardamom, angelica root, orris root, Thai lemon grass, pink peppercorn, kaffir lime leaf, mace, almond and lavender flower.

The LoneWolf Negroni

Ingredients
60ml LoneWolf Gin
30ml Campari
30ml sweet vermouth
Valencia orange peel to garnish

Method
Put all the ingredients in a mixer with ice and stir until well chilled.
Strain into a rocks glass, add a large cube of ice and garnish with a
twist of Valencia orange peel.

Vesperis Pictish Gin

Blackford Craft Distillery Ltd, Maryfield of Blackford,
Rothienorman, Inverurie AB51 8YL
www.blackfordcraftdistillery.co.uk
Price £38 / Quantity 700ml / ABV 40%

DEEP IN THE heart of what was once known as Pictland – that's the North East to you and me – lies a craft distillery that has gone back all the way to Roman times in search of inspiration for their gin.

Blackford Craft Distillery, a family-run production site, set up by Neil and Katie Sime in 2017, is based in a nineteenth-century steading that was once part of the Blackford Estate, with links to Fyvie Castle.

Maryfield Steading had been neglected until the Sime family took it over and sympathetically refurbished it into a still room and fully licensed distillery comprising of a plant room, excise warehouse, office and tasting room.

After launching their first spirit – Pictish Vodka – to great success, the Simes turned their attention to gin. They created their first offering using an ancient Pictish recipe for heather honey mead, which was originally brewed on the slopes on Bennachie, Aberdeenshire.

Designed to be a modern gin infused with 'ancient inspiration', Vesperis Pictish Gin uses the heather honey and heather blossom prevalent in the mead recipe as its primary botanicals.

The team have big aspirations. 2018 sees the launch of what they believe is Scotland's first Scottish honey vodka – the Vesperis Heather Honey Vodka, which uses Aberdeenshire heather honey from Udny Provender in Methlick and is based on a traditional Polish honey vodka, *krupnik*.

The Simes also have plans to release a fruit-infused gin and to begin exporting their gins to Europe. They hope to plant an orchard so that in a few years' time apples for the fruit gin will be grown on their own land.

Vesperis Pictish Gin

Vesperis Pictish Gin is made using local botanicals including raw heather honey, which is sourced from a local beekeeper, Udny Provender.

This is then combined with handpicked heather blossom from Royal Deeside and Bennachie, as well as seasonal apples from the orchards at Pitmedden Gardens and Kincardine Castle in Aberdeenshire. Together these create a 'completely unique' gin in which citrus and spice compete with a full floral finish from the heather.

The Picts historically observed the planets to track the seasons and they would carve their astronomical calendar – the V-Rod and Crescent – onto their standing stones.

To represent this, the logo on the bottle was designed with Mither Tap – one of the highest peaks of Bennachie – in the centre with Venus as the 'evening star' above it.

The gin itself takes its name from Vesper, the ancient name for the evening star.

Preferred serve

Over ice, served with premium tonic water and garnished with frozen raspberries.

Preferred garnish

Red fruit, particularly pomegranate or frozen raspberries.

Botanicals

Apples, heather honey, heather blossom, juniper berries, coriander seeds, lemon peel, angelica root and orris root.

Recommended cocktail

Pomegranate Martini

Red fruit and citrus really complement Pictish Gin without over-powering it. The subtle flavours of the juniper berries and coriander really come through along with the heather blossom finish, which is what gives this gin its special edge.

Ingredients
50ml Vesperis Pictish Gin
25ml triple sec
150ml fresh pomegranate juice
Orange zest to garnish

Method
Shake all the ingredients with ice, then strain into a martini glass and garnish with a curl of orange zest.

12 Kirsty's Gin

Arbikie Highland Estate Distillery, Inverkeilor, Arbroath DD11 4UZ
www.arbikie.com
Price £35 / *Quantity* 700ml / *ABV* 43%

HEAD NORTH FROM the central belt along the east coast towards Arbroath and the picturesque Lunan Bay, and you'll come across a unique highland estate. Nestled at the foot of the Angus hills, Arbikie is a working farm, which launched a spirits distillery on their grounds in 2014.

It was the brainchild of the estate's fourth-generation farmers, founders David, John and Iain Stirling. The brothers decided they wanted to revive 'field to bottle' distilling, taking produce grown on the farm and using it to create a diverse range of spirits that began with the creation of what is considered to be Scotland's first commercially available potato vodka.

They went on to produce several innovative vodkas, but it wasn't long before they moved into the category that would cement their reputation as one of Scotland's most fascinating drinks producers.

To get the project up and running, the brothers hired Heriot-Watt alumni Kirsty Black and Christian Perez-Solar as master distiller and production manager to oversee the creation and launch of the new distillery. Kirsty, who originally enrolled in the master's degree in Brewing and Distilling at Edinburgh University in a desire to learn more about brewing, is one of the only female master distillers in Scottish gin. She has played a large part in the creation of Arbikie's flagship expression, which is named after her as its creator.

The Angus-based distillers then followed up the release of their original bottling with a second gin, dubbed AK's.

With their keen interest in taking the gin from 'field to bottle', Arbikie are proud to do everything on site. This includes producing their own crops, with Scottish juniper soon to join the roster of plants cultivated on site.

Kirsty's Gin

Named after master distiller Kirsty Black, who developed it over a two-year period, Kirsty's Gin is described by commercial manager Adam Hunter as a 'traditional juniper-led floral gin'.

Designed to embody the elements – the sea, rock and land – which surround the two-thousand-acre estate as it stretches from the farm itself out to Lunan Bay on the east coast of Scotland, the gin uses the following three key botanicals.

Kelp (the element of the sea), carline thistle and blaeberries (the rock and land) were chosen primarily for their flavour, but also because they all grow wild in the Angus area and are ultimately sustainable – something Kirsty was very keen to incorporate into their gin production.

Another unique characteristic of Kirsty's Gin is that, unlike the majority of UK-produced gin, Arbikie's premier gin uses a potato vodka made on the estate as its base instead of grain neutral spirit. This gives it an intriguingly divergent profile – with Kirsty's Gin having what Arbikie describes as an 'extra smooth and distinctive' taste.

This potato vodka base is macerated with juniper and the key botanicals before being put through AK and Jan, Arbikie's stills, named after the Stirlings' parents. Kirsty's Gin is floral on the nose, with hints of pepper and summer fruits, smooth and refreshing on the finish with heavy flavours of juniper and citrus on the palate.

Preferred serve

In a tall glass filled with ice. Add a generous measure of Kirsty's Gin, top up with a quality tonic and add a garnish.

Preferred garnish

Some blueberries and a lemon twist. One stir with a bar spoon.

Basic garnish

A lemon twist. All the flavour in a lemon is contained within the oils of the skin, and by spraying the oils over the drink you release the floral notes in the gin, completely changing your Kirsty's gin and tonic.

Botanicals

Kelp, carline thistle, blaeberries, juniper, angelica, coriander, liquorice and orris.

Recommended cocktail

The Angus Breakfast

Adam says, 'This is my favourite Kirsty's Gin cocktail. It's simple to make at home and shows off the delicate flavours of Kirsty's Gin, highlighting the smoothness of the spirit. Not many gins are worthy of this cocktail.'

Ingredients
50ml Kirsty's Gin
25ml fresh lemon juice
Two spoonfuls of fine-cut marmalade
Grapefruit or orange twist

Method
Add all the ingredients to a shaker with ice, shake hard, double-strain into a chilled martini glass and garnish with a grapefruit or orange twist.

13

AK's Gin

Arbikie Highland Estate Distillery, Inverkeilor, Arbroath DD11 4UZ
www.arbikie.com
Price £35 / *Quantity* 700ml / *ABV* 43%

AK's Gin

This exciting gin was named after the father of the Arbikie founders and is made in honour of the man who inspired the three Stirling brothers to carry on the traditions of their family's farming roots.

Distilled using wheat farmed at the estate – from a field you can see from the distillery – Arbikie added black pepper, mace and cardamom as this drink's key ingredients to create a buttery, sweet gin.

This gin is made more special still by its use of sustainably sourced fresh Angus honey, thereby helping to preserve the UK's bee population and pollinate surrounding farmland.

AK's Gin is also a 2018 winner of the World's Best Martini award, defeating a number of leading international brands in collaboration with top London cocktail bar, The Gibson.

Recommended cocktail

AK's Alliance

Ingredients
35ml AK's Gin
20ml apricot liqueur
12.5ml lemon juice
12.5ml gomme syrup

Method
Shake and fine-strain into a chilled flute glass and top with Prosecco.
Garnish with dried apricot on the side of the glass to finish.

Verdant Dry Gin

Verdant Spirits Ltd, Edward Street Mill, Forest Park Place,
Dundee DD1 5NT
www.verdantspirits.co.uk
Price £34.95 / Quantity 700ml / ABV 43%

KNOWN AS THE city of jute, jam and journalism, Dundee is the birthplace of Desperate Dan, marmalade and the famous Antarctic expedition ship, the RRS *Discovery*.

Often overshadowed by Scotland's other cities, Dundee has undergone a cultural revolution in recent years and, spearheaded by the 2018 opening of the V&A museum, has found itself listed in numerous top travel guides such as Lonely Planet and influential publications like the *Wall Street Journal* as one of Europe's up-and-coming destinations.

The city is also home to the winner of the first ever 'Best Gin in Scotland' award. Verdant Dry Gin is the first release from Verdant Spirits, a company founded in April 2017 by Andrew Mackenzie – it also happens to be the first legal distillery in the city of discovery in nearly two hundred years.

Mixing tradition with modern techniques, the distillery is based in a former engine house of one of Dundee's old mills, which would once have housed some of the world's most cutting-edge industrial machinery.

As a mature student, Formula One industry veteran Mackenzie went back to university in Dundee to study a master's degree in Food and Drink Innovation and Technology, where he was inspired by a lecture by the current chair of the Scottish Craft Distillers Association, Alan Wolstenholme, on the spirits business.

Taking a keen interest in what he perceived as a gap in the market for quality spirits for the home cocktail market, Mackenzie undertook extensive market research and discussions with consumers to find out what they desired before he set about creating the first of a new range of spirits.

Distilled in small batches on their 500-litre still – named Little Eddie – Verdant Dry Gin is a nod to not only the classic style of gin but also the city's rich connection with the global trade routes of the past. Mackenzie chose each of this gin's ten botanicals specifically to give an overall flavour profile that's balanced and nuanced, allowing each ingredient their place in the final taste.

Most impressively, Verdant fought off competition from sixteen other contenders to take gold medal in the London Dry category at the Scottish Gin Awards 2017 before going on to win the judges' prize for the competition's best gin. Buoyed by such success, Mackenzie and his team are looking to build a shop and visitor centre at the distillery, as well as extending their spirits range to include rum, vodka and possibly whisky.

Verdant Dry Gin

Described as a classic London Dry gin, Verdant is designed to be as flavoursome as possible with rich top notes of juniper being followed by hits of citrus and an undercurrent of spice.

It's complex, full of flavour but still fresh tasting, but as Mackenzie explains, his gin is made with mixology in mind and features 'no gimmicks'.

Produced using ten botanicals, including grains of paradise, bitter orange, lemon peel and liquorice, this gin is perfect for those who enjoy best that traditional, juniper-led style.

Preferred serve

Either neat or with a premium tonic in a big glass, lots of ice and a wedge of lime or a twist of orange peel.

Preferred garnish

Verdant recommend a wedge of lime or a slice of orange peel, but they encourage people to be creative. For instance, Tom Kitchin serves Verdant with a cinnamon stick and some juniper.

Botanicals

Juniper, coriander seed, lemon peel, bitter orange, cassia bark, orris root, green cardamom, angelica, liquorice and grains of paradise.

Recommended cocktail

Verdant Dry Gin Elderflower Cosmopolitan

The cosmopolitan sprang to life in the 1980s but can trace its family tree right back to the gin gimlet, and even further to the classic 'Daisy'. Here, the addition of the elderflower liqueur adds a wonderful touch of sophistication to this perennial cocktail that still lets the full flavour of the Verdant shine through.

Ingredients
25ml Verdant Dry Gin
15ml triple sec
20ml elderflower liqueur
5ml fresh lime juice
35ml cranberry juice
Blood orange to garnish

Method
Place all the ingredients into a cocktail shaker and fill with ice. Shake well and then strain into a coupe or martini glass. Garnish with a slice of blood orange.

15

Kintyre Gin

Beinn an Tuirc Distillery, Lephincorrach Farm, Torrisdale,
Carradale, Campbeltown PA28 6QT
www.kintyregin.com
Price £36 / Quantity 70cl / ABV 43%

IT MIGHT NOT be the easiest distillery to get to, but the road trip becomes wholly worthwhile when you see the scenery. Set within the idyllic region of Kintyre and the Torrisdale Castle Estate, Beinn an Tuirc boasts magnificent views over the Kilbrannan Sound to the Isle of Arran.

The distillery itself is housed within a former piggery on the estate, which comprises around 1,200 acres of hills, forests and farmland and has been in the hands of the Macalister Hall family since 1872.

The unique rural setting is not the only asset that enables Beinn an Tuirc to stand out. These gin producers are also renowned for their focus on green energy and sustainability. The hill that gives the distillery its name – Beinn an Tuirc is Gaelic for 'hill of the wild boar' – provides the stream that is used by the hydro-electric scheme to power their German-imported copper still, which is rather delightfully named Big Don.

Launched in 2017 by the estate's laird Niall Macalister Hall, wife Emma and family dog Crumbles, this wonderful distillery has plans to launch a visitor centre. Firmly rooted in the local community, Beinn an Tuirc have pledged to plant a tree in their dedicated woodland area for every case of Kintyre Gin sold in a bid to minimise their impact on the environment. In addition, they invest a percentage of their profits in community projects and local business start-ups.

The distillery has created apple and bramble-flavoured gins and has also released an exciting gin aged in bourbon casks supplied by the nearby Glen Scotia Distillery.

Kintyre Gin

Created by head distiller Su Black using spring water from a well found on the estate, Kintyre Gin is described as having 'delicate floral notes and a citrus body, with a juniper and spice finish'.

It uses, among other botanicals, juniper, coriander and liquorice as well as Icelandic moss and sheep's sorrel, both of which have been chosen to reflect the countryside that surrounds the distillery.

Preferred serve

In a glass with Fever-Tree Mediterranean Tonic and garnished with a sprig of basil.

Preferred garnish

A sprig of basil.

Basic garnish

Fresh mint.

Botanicals

Juniper, coriander, angelica root, orris root, cubeb berries, almond, bitter orange peel, cassia bark, liquorice, lemon peel, Icelandic moss and sheep's sorrel.

Gintyre

Neil says, 'The Gintyre marries a sophisticated combination of sweet grenadine syrup with the aromatic citrus notes of Kintyre Gin.'

Ingredients
35ml Kintyre Gin
30ml grenadine
2 tsps pomegranate seeds, plus extra to garnish
Soda water

Method
Add the Kintyre Gin to a cocktail shaker followed by the grenadine. Throw in the fresh pomegranate seeds and shake over ice. Pour into a sugar-frosted martini glass, top up with soda water and garnish with more pomegranate seeds.

16
Hendrick's Gin

The Hendrick's Gin Distillery Ltd, The Girvan Distillery,
Girvan KA26 9PT
www.hendricksgin.com
Price £28 / *Quantity* 700ml / *ABV* 41.4%

TAKE A LONG meander south from Glasgow along the southwest coast of Scotland and you'll eventually reach the stunning vista of the Firth of Clyde with its striking view of Ailsa Craig. It's here you'll find, close the coastal town of Girvan, the home of Scotland's pioneering craft gin.

Lighting the torch paper – or firing the still, as it were – of the modern gin renaissance in Scotland, the decision by William Grant & Sons to release what would go on to become the first of Scotland's new craft gins, would turn out to be a master stroke.

Growing from minor experiments undertaken by Balvenie Malt Master Dave Stewart and distiller Lesley Gracie to a small release in 1999, Hendrick's has become one of the world's bestselling craft gin brands – topping one million cases sold in 2017. Strange to think that it took so long for the others to eventually catch on.

Gracie, whose ingenuity brought this unique juniper spirit to life, is now head distiller, ensuring Hendrick's is in safe hands. Working with a rare Bennett still from 1860 and a 1943 Carter-Head still bought by Charles Gordon, great-grandson of William Grant & Sons founder William Grant, at auction in 1966, Gracie still creates this hugely popular gin in relatively small batches.

Other than the unique way that it's distilled, Hendrick's strength is very much in the way it's marketed. Oozing Victoriana from every pore, the branding team very cleverly tied the gin to its now legendary garnish, the cucumber, so as to create a distinct serve and marking the gin as something from a different age.

Not to be undone by the rise of even more exaggerated garnishes, Hendrick's have stayed true to their original choice, even going as far as to back the annual Cucumber Day event on 14 June, which was established by cucumber growers in England in 2011 to highlight the pleasures of this versatile fruit.

The bottle itself is based on an old Victorian era apothecary's vial and features the year 1886 on its label, which is the year the first William Grant distillery was founded. While events such as an expedition to a

South American rainforest to search for a new botanical with which to create a gin and the creation of a night of music using cucumbers as instruments (yes really) have helped to tie the brand to a whimsical vision of Queen Victoria's reign – a major part of Hendrick's success.

Hendrick's Gin

Lesley Gracie, master distiller at Hendrick's, creates the gin using both of their unique stills to distil two separate heavier and lighter infused spirits which are then blended before the Bulgarian rose petal and specially selected cucumber essence are added post-distillation to create a rich, balanced juniper spirit.

The gin features several classic botanicals such as orris root, coriander seeds and citrus peel, alongside some more unusual ingredients including yarrow, chamomile and elderflower. The result is a gin that's smooth, full of depth and filled with subtle flavours; it's fresh, floral and bottled at a punchy 41.4% ABV.

With a price point that's often cheaper than many of the newer competitors to the market, and an availability that extends from most bar gantries to many supermarket shelves, Hendrick's is easily accessible and considered to be one of the best gins for beginners to find their feet in the category.

Preferred serve

Hendrick's curious flavour can produce some delightful cocktails. The traditionalists prefer a classic gin and tonic garnished with a cucumber slice, but there are a wealth of alternative preparation methods.

Preferred garnish

Hendrick's should be garnished with that humble yet marvellous green fruit – the cucumber. Three delicate rounds are perfect!

Botanicals

Orris root, yarrow, juniper, chamomile, lemon peel, orange peel, elderflower, angelica root, coriander seeds, cubeb berries and caraway seeds.

Recommended cocktail

Garibaldi Sbagliato

Ingredients
25ml Hendrick's Gin
25ml Campari
50ml fresh orange juice
Champagne
Orange wedge to garnish

Method
Combine all the ingredients in a frozen or chilled highball glass with no ice. Top with Champagne and garnish with an orange wedge.

Hills & Harbour Gin

Crafty Distillery, Wigtown Road, Newton Stewart DG8 6AS
www.craftydistillery.com
Price £38 / *Quantity* 700ml / *ABV* 40%

I N YEARS GONE by, the furthest south you could have found a local gin would have been Girvan, home of Hendrick's, but, as with the rest of Scotland, the south of the country now enjoys its fair share of outstanding gin distilleries and brands.

In Dumfries and Galloway, just south of the Galloway forest park and lying close to the flowing waters of the River Cree, you'll find the home of Hills & Harbour Gin and one of the country's most southerly spirit production sites, Crafty Distillery.

Founded in April 2014 by Graham Taylor, the custom-built distillery has enviable views over the Galloway countryside – and its premium gin is named after the terrain that surrounds the distillery. Filled with forests and unspoiled coastlines, these landscapes offer the 'perfect larder' in which to source ingredients.

The Crafty Distillery prides itself on removing all of what it calls 'distilling jargon' and 'trendy nonsense' to make their gin and distillery as approachable as possible. This ethos carries through into the way in which the distillery focuses on accessibility, with the small team offering a range of tours and master classes.

Key to this is the unique Galloway Gin Escape, in which guests can explore more of Galloway's stunning scenery while foraging for two of the distinctive local ingredients used in the gin. They can then learn how the spirit is made, sample some of the finished product and mix their own delicious cocktails.

Another intriguing aspect to Crafty is that they are one of the few Scottish distilleries to create their own base spirit. Wheat is taken from nearby farms to create a grain spirit that provides a smooth mouth feel and a delicate sweet flavour to the finished article.

Hills & Harbour Gin

With its grain spirit created from local wheat and botanicals chosen to result in a 'smooth and vibrant' gin, Hills & Harbour is ideal to drink neat, with a mixer or in a cocktail.

Chosen to mirror the forests and coastlines that give the area its distinct character, two of the botanicals – noble fir needles and bladderwrack seaweed – are foraged locally. Described as juniper-led with 'hints of forest fir, tropical fruit, citrus spice, tangy sherbet and a subtle scent of the shore', this beautifully versatile gin uses mango to add a depth and sweetness, and peppercorns to unify everything.

Preferred serve

A 50ml measure of Hills & Harbour Gin over plenty of ice, add some premium tonic and a slice of fresh mango to garnish.

Preferred garnish

A soft garnish like fresh mango.

Botanicals

Juniper, noble fir needles, bladderwrack seaweed, mango and peppercorns.

Galloway Forager

Ingredients
50ml Hills & Harbour Gin
25ml grapefruit oleo saccharum (made with molasses sugar)
25ml elderflower cordial
Soda water
A sprig of noble fir to garnish
A slice of grapefruit to garnish

Method
Fill a glass tumbler with ice, add the cocktail mix and top with a dash of soda. To serve, garnish with a fresh sprig of noble fir and a slice of fresh grapefruit.

18 Oro

Dalton Distillery, Dalton, Lockerbie DG11 1DU
www.orogin.co.uk
Price £38 / *Quantity* 700ml / *ABV* 43%

LYING SOUTH OF the picturesque town of Lockerbie and the River Annan, Dalton Distillery was created by the Clynick family in 2017. This idyllic rural setting is so rich with history that it seems almost anomalous to find one of the country's most cutting-edge gin distilleries here.

Ray Clynick, head distiller and co-founder, has a background as a scientist and, after graduating from Heriot-Watt International Centre for Brewing and Distilling, he set about working out how he and his family could create a gin based on a 'thoroughly scientific understanding' of how flavour compounds interact with each other.

As part of their research, they designed a bespoke copper still, which they named Bridie – after one of the family dogs – and the result is one of the most distinctive-looking stills you're likely to see. Replete with three partial condensers, the distilling set-up allows Ray and his team to control of every part of the process; it's versatile and creates as pure and clean a spirit as possible.

As part of their commitment to sustainability, the distillery uses locally collected rain water – in plentiful supply in Dumfries! – to cool the system. Unlike much of the distilling industry, the company doesn't produce any waste water.

Should you be curious about this fascinating new distillery, then the Clynicks will happily welcome you with a range of tours and tastings designed to show off what Dalton distillery is all about, as well as teaching you how to make the 'Perfectly Scientific Gin and Tonic'.

A 'classical style Scottish Dry Gin' Oro is the distillery's first release. The follow-up, Oro V, is a less traditional gin, which balances the juniper with the lighter, fresher notes of lavender.

Oro Gin

Aiming to create a gold standard in Scottish gins, the name of the gin means gold in both Spanish and Italian. The logo on Oro's bottle uses concentric circles to represent the atomic suborbital structure of gold itself. Oro is created using fifteen named botanicals including juniper, coriander, cinnamon, pink peppercorns and vanilla.

Ray and the team also use one signature ingredient, which they insist will 'for ever remain secret'.

Described as the first ever 'Scottish Dry Gin' by the Clynicks – owing to the fact that it's made to the strict rules of the London Dry category, but in a Scottish setting – Oro is very clean with its strong base of juniper followed by sweetness from the vanilla and subtle spices from the cinnamon and coriander.

Preferred serve

Simply, on the rocks. Oro is such a smooth gin that it really doesn't need a mixer.

Preferred garnish

A slice of lemon or a lavender flower.

Botanicals

Juniper, coriander, vanilla, orris root, lemon peel, orange peel, cassia bark, Malabar cardamom, pink peppercorns, lemongrass, angelica, fennel (smoothing agent), bitter almond, cinnamon, liquorice (smoothing agent) and one 'for ever secret' ingredient.

The Oro Martini

Ingredients
50–60ml strong Italian coffee
(the producers recommend Nespresso espresso forte)
40–50ml Oro Gin
10ml Monin gomme syrup
Ice
Coffee beans to garnish

Method
Fill your cocktail shaker with ice, then pour the coffee, gin and syrup on top. Shake hard for twelve seconds – you want the ice to break up a bit, which will chill the drink and create that lovely frothy top. Then double-strain into a coupe or martini glass. Garnish with a few coffee beans.

19 Lilliard

Lilliard Ginnery, Born in the Borders, Lanton Mill, Jedburgh TD8 6ST
www.lilliardgin.co.uk
Price £32 / *Quantity* 700ml / *ABV* 40%

THE ROLLING AGRICULTURAL lands of the Scottish Borders provide a bountiful supply of amazing foodstuffs and beautifully made craft products, but, up until a few years ago, you would have struggled to find any kind of local spirit or beer to slake your thirst.

Now the region has come alive with some exhilarating new businesses launching gins, laying down whisky spirit in casks and investigating the possibilities of even more expansive drinks like rum.

One such distiller, which narrowly missed out in the race to become the first to produce gin in the region in centuries, is Lilliard. This small craft producer is firmly embedded in the Borders region, specifically the Teviot Valley.

Launched in February 2017, the gin is named for the heroine of the Battle of Ancrum Moor, fought just outside the village in 1545. The tale tells how Lilliard took up her sword against Henry VIII's army and fought to the death to avenge the murder of her lover at the English army's hands. Part of the Teviot Valley, where the gin is based, now bears her name, and it seemed only fitting that this gin should be named in honour of her indomitable spirit.

Based at Born in the Borders, side-by-side with the successful brewery there, the Lilliard Ginnery uses locally foraged botanicals which are chosen to reflect the vibrant rural landscapes of the Borders. Given its eponymous heroine, it's interesting that the team has disavowed the traditional naming conventions – in the interests of gender equality – to name their still after a man, with Donald being their chosen moniker (and, no, not that Donald).

As a fully interactive location, the Born in the Borders ethos is also reflected in the Ginnery where you'll find micro-tours and gin classes.

Lilliard Gin

Rowan, rosehip, meadowsweet and elderflower are used to make Lilliard gin; these all grow around the distillery, creating a vivid snapshot of the Borders terroir. Other more traditional botanicals include juniper, angelica and a couple of different types of orange.

Designed to capture and convey the fragrant floral valleys of the Scottish Borders at midsummer, Lilliard is a classic dry gin, but with a 'contemporary floral twist'.

Preferred serve

Fever-Tree Naturally Light Tonic, and a slice of orange peel.

Preferred garnish

Orange peel.

Botanicals

Rosehip, rowan, meadowsweet, juniper, angelica, liquorice, orange peel and elderflower.

The Maiden's Prayer

Ingredients
1 measure Lilliard Gin
1 measure triple sec
1 tsp orange juice
1 tsp lemon juice
A twist of lemon to garnish

Method
Shake all of the ingredients over ice, then strain into a cocktail
glass and garnish with a lemon twist.

The Crow Man's Gin

The Kelso Gin Company, Ancrum, Jedburgh TD8 6UQ
www.kelsoginco.com
Price £42.50 / Quantity 70cl / ABV 40%

WINNING THE RACE to become the first new distillery in the Borders for over one hundred and eighty years, Kelso Gin Company was launched in 2016 by businessman Robert Armstrong, investor Oliver Drake and distiller Andrew Crow.

With a focus on using botanicals that reflect the rich history and bountiful nature of the Borders and the region in which the distillery was conceived, the micro-distillery uses only organic grain spirit. And, perhaps most intriguingly, it doesn't redistill the head and tails – the impure cast-off cuts which still contains alcohol – as other distilleries do; instead, a far slower triple distillation process creates a smoother gin.

Located close to the River Tweed, the brand launched with three gins, the Kelso Elephant, a spiced gin, the Crow Man's Gin, their traditional dry gin with a cardamom twist, and the Crow Man's Lovage Gin, which is made using herbs sourced locally from the Teviot Valley. The team says the latter has a flavour 'that's to die for'.

Armstrong, whose family have a rich background in distilling, says the brand's mascot, the Crow Man, was inspired by a local legend of the travelling seventeenth-century medicine man – and most decidedly not the Worzel Gummidge character. This character would fill the large nose on his distinctive mask with preventative herbs and spices in a bid to prevent him catching the sicknesses of others. Dressed this way, he would tour the local area offering the afflicted his cures and remedies – made from special blends of herbs, spices and secret ingredients – from his leather bag.

Fitting then that head distiller Andrew Crow – also partly the inspiration for the Crow Man – has become a more modern version of his namesake, offering the weary, the tired and the stressed respite in the form of his own legendary juniper concoctions and even going as far as to don the outfit of the plague doctor for special tastings and deliveries.

Crow and the team have also produced several seasonal flavoured gins, including dead nettle, raspberry, elderflower and rhubarb, as well as a limited edition 'St Abbs Lifeboat Gin' made with locally foraged botanicals including kelp from St Abbs, the profits of which go to the St Abbs Independent Lifeboat Charity.

Not ones to sit back and relax, the Kelso stable expanded their spirits range with a quadruple-distilled vodka dubbed Wojciech, inspired by the Polish bear of the same name – Wojtek – who became famous during the Second World War for assisting the Allied war effort. There's a memorial to Wojtek in Princes Street Gardens, Edinburgh, if you fancy learning more about this extraordinary soldier bear.

The Crow Man's Gin

Created using traditional gin stalwarts such as juniper, cinnamon, angelica and several other 'secret botanicals', Crow Man's Gin is 'exceptionally smooth', and interestingly 'creamy' owing to its thicker mouth feel.

Powerful hits of juniper add to the punch of this gin, which is as enjoyable on its own over ice as it is with a mixer such as soda or tonic.

Preferred serve

Try over ice first then experiment with different mixers. Andrew believes it's such a versatile gin that it will work with anything.

Preferred garnish

A wedge of lime.

Botanicals

Juniper, cinnamon, allspice, angelica and other 'secret ingredients'.

Recommended cocktail

The Crow Man's Gin Sling

Ingredients
50ml Crow Man's Gin
½ tsp of sugar
10ml lemon juice
Soda
Lemon twist to garnish

Method
Shake the gin, sugar and lemon juice in a cocktail shaker with ice
and then strain into an ice-filled glass, top with the soda and add the
lemon twist for garnish.

Darnley's Gin

Darnley's Distillery, East Newhall Farm, Kingsbarns, Fife KY16 8QE
www.darnleysgin.com
Price £32.99 / *Quantity* 700ml / *ABV* 42.7%

AFTER BEING CONTRACT distilled in London, Darnley's Gin – previously known as Darnley's View Gin – enjoyed something of a homecoming in 2017. It returned to Fife and the East Neuk – the traditional home of owners, the Wemyss family – where it is now housed in a small farm cottage found on the grounds of its sister distillery, Kingsbarns, which produces single malt whisky.

Born of the Wemyss family's passion for spirits, Darnley's is the result of their background in whisky and wine, but also their fascination with the endless combination of botanicals you can use in gin making and the impact this has on flavour.

This led to their first gin being launched in 2010, named in celebration of the moment that Mary Queen of Scots first spied her husband-to-be Lord Darnley at Wemyss Castle in 1565. Interestingly, their marriage would go on to produce James I of England and VI of Scotland, the first king to preside over the union between England and Scotland. This connection between the two countries is now reflected in the story of Darnley's Gin.

The gin underwent a rebranding in 2017, with the word 'view' being dropped from the label. The packaging was also updated to reflect a more modern approach, with sketchings of the botanicals added and the labelling pared back.

Darnley's core range now features three main gins – Original, Spiced, and Spiced Navy Strength – and a limited edition range dubbed the Cottage series, most of which are now made in their Italian copper stills, with a Fife local, Scott Gowans, as the gin distiller heading up production.

Darnley's Spiced Gin

Darnley's Gin is made in a traditional pot still using the London Dry method, and though the original is a great example of the style, the spiced gin – launched in 2012 – intrigues with its own particular *je ne sais quoi*.

While its predecessor was inspired by the elderflower that grows wild around the Wemyss family estate in Scotland, the spiced version is influenced by a faraway range of global flavours. Featuring the usual players such as juniper, angelica and coriander, the spiced gin also contains the tastes of South Asia and West Africa. Ingredients such as nutmeg, clove and grains of paradise give it a wonderfully rich flavour that sets it apart in an enticingly distinctive way from many of its competitors.

Preferred serve

In a tall glass with ice and ginger ale, garnished with a slice of orange.

Preferred garnish

A slice of orange.

Botanicals

Juniper, cinnamon, cassia, angelica, coriander, nutmeg, clove, cumin, ginger and grains of paradise.

Recommended cocktail

Red Snapper

Ingredients
50ml Darnley's Spiced Gin
75ml tomato juice
10ml fresh orange juice
Juice of half a lime
3 dashes of Tabasco sauce (to taste)
2 tsps Worcestershire Sauce
2 grinds of cracked black pepper
2 tsps fino sherry
Celery salt
A celery stick to garnish

Method
Run a lime wedge around the rim of the glass and then dip the wet rim into the celery salt. Fill the glass with cubed ice then pour in the gin, tomato, lime and orange juices and the Tabasco and Worcestershire sauces. Float the sherry on top and grind black pepper over the top too. Garnish with a celery stick.

Eden Mill Love Gin

Eden Mill Distillery, Main St, Guardbridge,
St Andrews KY16 0UU
www.edenmill.com
Price £30 / *Quantity* 500ml / *ABV* 42%

BUOYED BY THE success of their beer and gin, St Andrews' own Eden Mill, which can be found close to the site of the old Seggie Distillery on the banks of the River Eden, has plans in place for a multimillion pound expansion. This will see a former paper mill in Guardbridge transformed into a state-of-the-art brewery and distillery.

Not one for resting on his laurels, founder Paul Miller followed this news with the release of the distillery's first single malt whisky. This marked the end of the journey that saw them lay down their first casks in 2015; it also cemented their place as Scotland's first true single-site brewery and distillery, with the country's triumvirate of drinks – whisky, beer and gin – all produced on the one site.

Eden Mill is also leading the charge when it comes to gin tourism. The site has around 25,000 visitors a year and, on top of the tours they offer, they have launched the Blendworks, a gin blending master class at the nearby Rusacks Hotel, St Andrews, which overlooks the iconic eighteenth hole of the Old Course. This tasting and gin-making course, as well as educating guests on the history of gin, is a great way to discover this innovative and multi-faceted spirit.

Starting life as a craft brewer in 2012, the company expanded into spirits in late 2014 with the launch of its original gin, created using an intriguing botanical – sea buckthorn berries sourced in Fife – and quickly followed up with a hop gin, which alluded to their connection between brewing and gin making using Australian galaxy hops as one of its main botanicals.

The Oak gin, which is made using oak chips to mellow out the flavour, was also added to their core range soon after. Other seasonal specials followed, including a nod to St Andrews and its links to golf with a gin made using hickory wood, which is traditionally used to make golf clubs. But it's Eden Mill's Love Gin, released for Valentine's Day 2015, that is the focus here thanks to its popularity, distinctive flavour and characteristics.

Eden Mill Love Gin

The first thing you'll notice about any Eden Mill gin is that it comes in their attractive ceramic bottles with their fun swing-top stoppers – readers of a certain age will remember liberating these from empty Grolsch bottles to become fashion accessories.

And the Love Gin is no different. It's described as the ideal gift for any gin fan on special occasions – in particular, Valentine's Day – but it really comes into its own on a warm summer's day when its deliciously fruity flavour adds just the right level of refreshment to a mixed drink.

Featuring rose petals, marshmallow root, goji berries, rhubarb root and hibiscus flowers, as well as some of the more classic gin botanicals, the Love Gin has a floral taste with warm berry notes, which along with its lovely pinky colour means the gin appeals to the eyes almost as much as to the nose and taste buds.

Preferred serve

In a glass with ice and Fentiman's rose lemonade.

Preferred garnish

Grapefruit or raspberry.

Botanicals

Juniper, coriander seed, angelica, rose petal, elderberry, rhubarb root, marshmallow root, goji berry, raspberry leaf and whole hibiscus flowers.

French Kiss

Ingredients
25ml Eden Mill Love Gin
25ml Eden Mill Strawberry & Black Pepper Liqueur
25ml strawberry cordial
Dash of lemon juice
25ml absinthe
Laurent-Perrier Champagne
Fresh strawberries to garnish

Method
Combine the gin, liqueur, cordial, lemon juice and absinthe, and shake well in a mixer before straining into a champagne flute and topping with Laurent-Perrier Champagne. Garnish with a fresh strawberry.

Avva Scottish Gin

Moray Distillery Ltd, 10 Chanonry Road North, Elgin IV30 6NF
www.moraydistilleryltd.co.uk
Price £38 / *Quantity* 700ml / *ABV* 43%

THE SPEYSIDE REGION is, of course, world famous for its whisky production. However, thanks to the Elgin-based Moray Distillery and Avva Gin – launched by drinks industry veteran Jill Brown in 2016 – the area now holds its own in Scotland's burgeoning gin scene.

The creation of the distillery came at the end of a six-year journey, which, Brown explains, was the result of a long time spent planning and building up the courage to action those plans. A one-woman show, the Moray Distillery is, much like the fifty or so whisky distilleries that neighbour it, very much rooted to the land and community in which it is based.

Moray is one of the only Scottish gin distilleries to have a Scottish-made still – which was especially crafted at the Speyside Copperworks. Brown named this bespoke copper still Jessie Jean – or J.J. for short – after her grandmothers.

The Speyside connection can also be seen in the brand's choice of botanicals. Nearly half of those used to make Avva Gin are foraged in the area and, perhaps more poignantly, all were 'weeds' the distiller says she originally found growing on her grandparents' farm.

And, of course, no Speyside venture would be complete without a connection to the spirit that is so deeply rooted in the region. Thus, in 2017, Moray Distillery released a gin matured in a whisky cask. The former bourbon cask used to age the special gin was chosen in clear homage to Speyside whisky; many of the distillery's neighbours use these particular barrels to mature their new-make spirit.

The name Avva was chosen for the fact that it means 'respected grandmother' or 'respectable elder woman' in the Indian language of Dravidian, while in Hebrew it apparently means to 'overturn or ruin', which is a cheeky nod to the spirit's age-old moniker 'mother's ruin'.

Avva Gin

Avva Gin is known for being very smooth and, like its neighbouring single malts, can be drunk over ice without a mixer. A London-style dry gin, it's a 'clean finish, well-balanced' example of the style, which has proved hugely popular since its launch in 2016.

A single shot, small-batch – one hundred and twenty litres – and vapour-basket-distilled gin, Avva is created using eleven botanicals with five of them coming from the area around the distillery. The dandelion, nettle, mint, red clover and rowan berries – which Brown says comes from her friend's farm outside Dufftown – are all foraged from Caithness down to Speyside.

The focus and careful planning that went into creating Avva's flagship spirit can also be seen in the branding. The bottle that carries the gin was created in tribute to a local landmark once known as the 'Lantern of the North', the Elgin Cathedral. The logo design references the building's famous rose window – which also appears on the large cork stopper – and the arched windows form the label's background.

Preferred serve

Straight over ice with a slice of lime or red apple.

Preferred garnish

A slice of red apple.

Basic garnish

A slice of lime.

Botanicals

Juniper, coriander seed, angelica root, orris root, rowan berries, dandelion, red clover, mint, nettles and citrus peel including lemon and orange.

Recommended cocktail

Avva Bax-Star Martini

This is a twist on the Pornstar Martini, which uses the Mango & Passion Fruit Curd made by Avva Gin's neighbours, Baxters.

Ingredients
35ml gin
1 good heaped spoon of Baxters Mango & Passion Fruit Curd
Squeeze of lime
Tonic or Prosecco

Method
Load a shaker with ice and the gin, curd and lime – shake hard and fast to ensure the curd mixes through. Strain into a chilled martini glass and top with tonic or Prosecco.

24 Badachro Gin

Badachro Distillery, Aird Hill, Badachro, Wester Ross IV21 2AB
www.badachrodistillery.com
Price £36.95 / *Quantity* 700ml / *ABV* 42.2%

THE TALE OF Badachro is one of serendipity as much as it is one of provenance, and of the lasting relationships between people and place.

An inn in a former fishing village close to the spectacular Loch Gairloch in the Northwest Highlands was the scene of the first meeting between Gordon and Vanessa Quinn. The couple went on to marry and then, eventually, by way of the Middle East and London, set up a bed and breakfast that would form the beginnings of their distillery.

Tired of the rat race, Gordon and horticulturalist wife Vanessa returned to Badachro to build themselves a new home and a life in the area where they first met. In a desire to create a keepsake for the tourists who visited their bed and breakfast, the pair decided to create a gin that that was 'truly of Badachro', something for guests to take home as an authentic expression of the place.

Vanessa, who Gordon describes as the more creative of the pair, turned an old joke about Badachro being so special 'because of the smells' on its head and that became their inspiration.

Instead she pointed out that the region is actually filled with lovely smells such as the sea breeze, the gorse blossoms in the summer, and the wild myrtle after the rain.

The couple decided to take this idea forward, thinking that if they could bottle these wonderful smells they could create their keepsake. First, they experimented with a myrtle liqueur – *Mirto*, a drink popular in Italy – then a flavoured vodka, before settling on what would become their gin, which they launched in spring 2017.

A family affair, the distilling is presided over by Gordon while Vanessa leads the foraging and takes care of recipe development and quality standards, which the children, Sean and Ashley, help out with wherever possible.

Badachro Gin

The couple handpicks the botanicals such as myrtle, elderflower, lavender, rosehip and gorse blossom from within five hundred metres of the distillery but, as Gordon explains, while they would love to pick their own juniper it doesn't grow abundantly on the west coast because of the climate. Instead, they source most of it from Croatia and Italy and combine it with the handpicked plants and traditional gin botanicals such as liquorice roots, orris roots, angelica, citrus, lemongrass and lime leaves to create their gin. The lime leaves are there after experiments with citrus peels resulted in slight hints of bitterness.

The resulting gin is not your typical flat-profiled London Dry gin. It's full flavoured, quite fruity to start with, spicy and sweeter in the middle with the juniper and myrtle and, at the end, there are citrus notes with the possibility of picking up on the lavender.

Preferred serve

Badachro is gaining quite a reputation as a sipping gin. It's perfect to enjoy with tonic and a garnish of a slice of lime and cardamom pod – not crushed or bruised – which adds a pleasing dryness to the finish.

Preferred garnish

A slice of lime and a cardamon pod.

Botanicals

Juniper, myrtle, elderflower, lavender, rosehip, gorse blossom, liquorice roots, orris roots, angelica, citrus, lemongrass and lime leaves.

Badachro Bramble

The Quinn family make their own cassis and use it to create their
distinctive version of a bramble.

Ingredients
50ml Badachro Gin
25ml freshly squeezed lemon or lime juice
25ml sugar syrup
25ml crème de cassis (Badachro's own or otherwise)

Method
Mix it all together in a shaker and pour over ice.

25

Caorunn

Balmenach Distillery, Balmenach Rd, Cromdale,
Grantown-on-Spey PH26 3PF
www.caorunngin.com
Price £29 / *Quantity* 700ml / *ABV* 41.8%

PROOF OF THE idea that you don't have to be a new distillery to take advantage of being able to make both whisky and gin, Speyside's Balmenach Distillery brought specialist equipment to their site in 2008 before beginning production of the juniper spirit alongside their whisky in May 2009.

Forming part of the big three Scottish craft gins alongside the Botanist and Hendrick's, Caorunn – pronounced 'ka-roon' – played a huge part in driving this category forward and it should take a lot of the credit for its success. Its name comes from the Gaelic word for one of Caorunn's most important botanicals, the rowan berry.

Gin Master Simon Buley, who also happens to be the assistant manager at Balmenach Distillery, explained that the link with whisky production helps in some ways – such as nosing, tasting and quality control – but the distilling technique used to produce the gin is so unique that it takes a fair amount of adjustment to master it.

The specialist equipment – supplied by the former owners of Inverhouse Distillers – comes in the form of an original hundred-year-old copper berry chamber. This has been adapted from its original use – which was to make perfume.

Buley believes that their unique system of vapour infusion, which sees the eleven botanicals placed in four baskets within the copper still, helps to create a light, supremely balanced spirit with the copper contact helping to strip away some of the harsher flavours. Buley's aim is that Caorunn should 'distil the Scottish Highlands into a glass': it's a drink made to directly reflect the area in which it is produced.

The distillery itself offers an in-depth behind-the-scenes tour of their production area, along with a tutored deconstructed nosing and tasting session, finishing off with a refreshing Caorunn and tonic with crisp red apple wedges in their innovative bothy.

Coarunn Gin

Caorunn is made using eleven botanicals; five of which are specifically selected owing to their use throughout Celtic history for medicinal purposes. All five of these locally sourced wild botanicals grow within a five-minute walk of the distillery.

The team use heather, which grows on the hills around the distillery; Coul Blush apples, which originated in the 1800s in Coul, Ross-shire; bog myrtle, which grows next to the heather and, rather delightfully, is also used for midge repellent; dandelion leaves and the eponymous rowan berry.

These are then added to the juniper and five other traditional botanicals to create a clean, crisp, fruity and slightly floral gin that is well rounded with no one flavour taking too much of a lead.

Preferred serve

Gin and tonic with a red apple garnish.

Preferred garnish

A slice of red apple.

Botanicals

Juniper, coriander seeds, lemon peel, orange peel, angelica root, cassia bark, heather, rowan berries, Coul Blush apples, bog myrtle and dandelion leaves.

Apple Winter Toddy

Ingredients
45ml Caorunn Gin
125ml cloudy apple juice
Dash of port
20ml lemon juice
2 tsps caster sugar
2 dashes of Angostura bitters
Orange slice with cloves to garnish
Slices of red apple to garnish
Grated nutmeg

Method
Add the ingredients together, stir with a spoon then heat in a pan over a stove for a few minutes. Once hot but not boiling, pour into a glass and garnish with a clove-studded orange slice, a few slices of red apple and grated nutmeg.

Devil's Staircase

Pixel Spirits Ltd, Old Ferry Road, North Ballachulish,
Fort William PH33 6SA
www.pixelspiritsltd.co.uk
Price £39 / *Quantity* 700ml / *ABV* 42%

NOT CONTENT WITH buying and running a small hotel bar and restaurant in what is some of the most breathtaking scenery the country has to offer – the Western Highlands and the Grampian Mountains – Craig and Noru Innes decided to build their own gin distillery.

Loch Leven Hotel, which sits on the northern shore of Loch Leven, is now home to Pixel Spirits and the location of one of the country's newest craft distilleries and gin schools.

The journey towards gin production began for the pair when they decided to commission a branded gin for the bar. Having contacted a few contract distillers to no avail, they decided to simply do it themselves.

The construction of the new distillery began in an almost derelict seventeenth-century A-frame barn – part of croft buildings currently on the grounds of Loch Leven Hotel – in 2015. Craig, the master distiller, along with another member of the hotel's staff, who happened to be a carpenter, completed the build in October 2017. All the work was done in-house with only the electrics and more complicated plumbing jobs outsourced to local tradespeople.

The first batch of Devil's Staircase, named for the ominous, outrageously steep off-road track that's part of the West Highland Way, was created just a few months later. Made in small batches, Devil's Staircase is handcrafted from hand-foraged botanicals on their still, affectionately named 'Orsetta' – Italian for 'little bear' – from start to finish, with each bottle hand-signed and numbered by Craig.

A limited edition Highland Dry gin called Neptune's Staircase followed, only three batches of which were ever distilled, and the husband and wife team are passionate about introducing a further range of gins and spirits as the business expands.

They share this passion for gin at their school, where fellow enthusiasts can learn the art of distilling on traditional copper pot mini-stills and create their own gin recipes. Located within the historic former byre of the distillery, the school is open to gin fans from absolute beginner to expert, with each guest taking home a bottle of their creation upon completion of the five-hour experience.

Devil's Staircase Gin

Craig describes the Devil's Staircase as the 'perfect blend of warm spice and citrus zest' with ten botanicals used to create the refreshingly sweet (juniper, coriander, orange peel and lemon peel) and spicy (the grains of paradise, cardamom, nutmeg and cassia) profile of this fun Highland spiced gin.

Each gin is truly small batch, with less than eighty bottles per batch, with a label featuring a fun illustration of a red devil beginning his ascent of a stone staircase, reflecting the rugged trek that gives the gin its name.

Preferred serve

With a premium Scottish tonic such as Walter Gregor's, over ice with a little fresh orange peel and a cardamom pod or two. However, Craig reckons it also goes extremely well with ginger ale, stating that there's something about the 'warmth of flavours that just sits so perfectly with the ginger'.

Preferred garnish

A ribbon of orange peel and a couple of cardamom pods.

Botanicals

Juniper, coriander, angelica, orris, orange peel, lemon peel, grains of paradise, cardamom, nutmeg and cassia.

The Spiced Bee's Knees

This is the producer's take on a Prohibition-era classic – the bee's knees. It's the perfect summer serve: the spice from the gin and sweetness of the honey balanced with the acidity of the citrus make it the ultimate refreshing cocktail.

Ingredients
50ml Devil's Staircase Gin
2 tsps Ed's Bees Glasgow Honey (or other pure honey)
20ml freshly squeezed lemon juice
20ml freshly squeezed orange juice
Orange peel and a couple of cardamom pods for garnish

Method
Chill a cocktail glass. In the bottom of a cocktail shaker, add the gin and honey and stir until the honey has dissolved, then add the freshly squeezed orange and lemon juices and shake over ice for twenty seconds to chill the drink. Discard the ice from the glass and strain the cocktail straight into the glass. Garnish with an orange peel and a couple of cardamom pods to serve.

27

GlenWyvis GoodWill Gin

GlenWyvis Distillery, Upper Docharty, Dingwall IV15 9UF
www.glenwyvis.com
Price £36.99 / *Quantity* 700ml / *ABV* 40%

SITTING PROUDLY UPON a hill overlooking Dingwall and the Cromarty Firth, with the stunning backdrop of the Ben Wyvis mountainside, GlenWyvis is considered to be Scotland's first community-owned distillery, with over 3,200 owners, all of whom put money towards its creation.

A community-benefit society, which means a share of all future profits will be invested back into community projects both locally and further afield, people from thirty-two countries have invested over £3 million to join the fledgling distillery group on their journey.

Dingwall's last whisky distillery closed in 1926, and, almost a century later, its successor, the new GlenWyvis spirits production site began producing its own spirit on Burns Night 2018.

Led by master distiller Duncan Tait, who brings twenty-six years of experience in the drinks industry, and founder and managing director John McKenzie, the team hopes that the new project will regenerate the town, create jobs and, in the long term, see the profits being passed onto other worthwhile community schemes.

The distillery, keen to push sustainability, takes water straight from Ben Wyvis into their on-site bore hole and uses renewable energy sources such as wind, hydro, solar and biomass.

Previously, their Highland gin had been made at Strathearn Distillery in Perthshire – as the liquid produced at the Dingwall site was originally being used only to make spirit for the whisky. However, the team installed their new gin still – affectionately named Heather – in summer 2018, bringing the production process home and creating this new gin in the process.

Made using nine botanicals, including spices, fruits and locally picked hawthorn berries, GoodWill Gin is the first major release from this brilliant craft distillery.

Already laying down spirit in casks for whisky and, sitting as it is on the route of the North Coast 500, the GlenWyvis team celebrated their connection as the only dual distillery on the route by creating a special limited edition NC500 gin.

GlenWyvis GoodWill Gin

'Made to share', GoodWill Gin comes in a fantastic bottle with a low curved neck and striking purple label which is embossed with icons relating to its creation.

GoodWill has a crisp, full-bodied taste with distinct hints of citrus from the orange and lemon, followed by the spiced warmth from the coriander and cinnamon.

It's an invigorating gin that not only tastes great, but also helps to provide money towards strengthening and improving a Highland community. You can feel good about yourself while drinking GoodWill.

Preferred serve

Over ice, with Fever-Tree Premium Tonic Water (or if you're feeling bold, Fever-Tree Elderflower Tonic Water) with toasted orange peel and bruised coriander leaves.

Preferred garnish

Toasted orange peel and bruised coriander leaves.

Botanicals

Juniper, orange peel, lemon peel, almond powder, orris root, hawthorn berries, cinnamon stick, coriander seeds and angelica root.

Recommended cocktail

The GlenWyvis

Ingredients
50ml GoodWill Gin
25ml lemon juice
10ml Bénédictine D.O.M.
10ml orgeat syrup
10ml ginger syrup
1 tsp orange marmalade

Method
Shake all the ingredients in a shaker until chilled (approximately fifteen seconds) and then double-strain over crushed ice.

28

Inshriach

Inshriach Distillery, Inshriach House, Inshriach, Aviemore PH22 1QP
www.inshriachgin.com
Price £38 / *Quantity* 700ml / *ABV* 40%

SET DEEP IN the heart of the Cairngorms National Park and located between the River Spey, Loch Insh and the foothills of the Cairngorms, in two hundred acres of woodland, Inshriach House lends its grounds and its name to an enticing Speyside gin.

The distillery itself came to the attention of the public in 2015 when it won Channel 4's Shed of the Year and helped to launch a hugely successful gin in Crossbill. Now, with a new set-up and a new team, the distillery has relaunched its own Original and Navy Strength gins.

Originally founded by Walter Micklethwait, everything used in the gin is picked within five miles of the grounds. A one-man operation, Walter enlists the help of volunteers when it comes to harvesting time because the window when the ingredients are 'just right' is relatively narrow.

The region is one of the few remaining strongholds of Scottish juniper, and as Walter points out, it is also an area abundant in 'interesting and edible botany'. The wild juniper itself grows all around Inshriach, with Walter freezing the berries to keep their flavour after his army of volunteers has helped in the harvest.

Only two other botanicals are then collected: the rosehip, which is found close to the juniper in the Spey valley, while the Douglas fir is taken from the nearby forest. Even the water is sourced from a spring on the hill behind the estate adding its own distinctively fresh flavour.

The shed itself is reminiscent of a frontier building from a spaghetti western and is locally sourced and mostly recycled, making Inshriach an extremely low-impact business.

The first edition of Inshriach was launched in February 2017, with the latest being the ninth edition. Each batch varies slightly because of independent factors.

The shed is not normally open to visitors, but community is important to Walter, meaning he holds the occasional open day – or as the distiller calls it 'a mini-festival' – where people can enjoy food, music, gin and plenty of cocktails. They also host botany and foraging weekends once or twice a year, allowing their fans to explore the grounds and learn all about the pivotal plants and berries that go into Inshriach's making.

Inshriach Original Gin

Made in very small batches of just five hundred or one thousand, the gin itself comes with a beautifully simple label reflecting the rustic nature of the distillery itself. The ABV is writ large on the front and the batch number handwritten on the bottom.

With evocative floral sweetness and strong hints of that fresh Scottish juniper, Walter describes his gin as 'the equivalent of walking in the forest – fresh and clear and airy but juniper forward with pine and sweetness'.

The three components offer their own flavours in an excellent balance and this makes it perfect for drinking neat over ice though it is robust enough to make an excellent gin and tonic.

Preferred serve

Neat on the rocks, perhaps with a tiny squeeze of lemon or with a slimline tonic.

Preferred garnish

A twist of lemon peel.

Botanicals

Juniper berries and sometimes tips at the right time of year, rosehips and Douglas fir.

Recommended cocktail

White Lady

Ingredients
35ml Inshriach Gin
10ml Cointreau
25ml lemon juice
10ml sugar syrup
Lemon peel to garnish

Method
Fill the shaker with ice and add the ingredients, shake until cold then strain into a coupe glass. Garnish with a twist of lemon peel.

29

Loch Ness Gin

Loch Ness Spirits Ltd, Athbhinn, Inverness IV2 6TU
www.lochnessgin.co.uk
Price £45 / *Quantity* 700ml / *ABV* 43.3%

LYING JUST SOUTH of Inverness on the north-eastern bank of Scotland's most famous loch is a spirits company that aims to create a gin that will become as notorious as the monster that haunts the waters and can be found snaking its way up its label.

Loch Ness Gin was launched in August 2016 by Kevin Cameron-Ross and his wife, local GP Lorien Cameron-Ross, whose family has lived in the area for over five hundred years. Lorien speaks of how the bones of her ancestors are 'literally lying in the ground' that grows their botanicals.

Talking of which, the pair keep the botanicals they use as a closely guarded secret. Though they enjoy affecting an air of mystery very much in keeping with the loch that gives their gin its name, Lorien adds that the real reason for the secrecy is to ensure customers can make their own judgements as to the taste profile.

Even with this reluctance to disclose their recipe, the Cameron-Rosses are happy to explain that all the botanicals they use are sourced close to the distillery, handpicked on the banks of Loch Ness. These include the abundant 'black gold' juniper, which they gather from their own crop. It's the beauty of this which led them to create their own gin.

The entrepreneurial pair credits the advice and guidance given to them by fellow Scottish distillers for the fact that their gin so quickly grew into a viable product that now flies off the shelves.

Loch Ness Gin is made in four annual batches of just five hundred at a time, owing to the availability not only of their rare native crop of juniper, but also other local botanicals sustainably sourced from the area. The gin is then hand-bottled and hand-labelled on site.

Looking to the future, the pair confirms they are working on a new gin to add to their range and will soon launch their own absinthe and vodka too.

Loch Ness Gin

Hand-distilled in a 50-litre still, Loch Ness Gin has won multiple awards since its release. Produced in small batches, it's lauded as a premium gin with 'perfumed floral aromas combined with delightful fruity notes and just a hint of pine'.

The packaging is as intriguing as the gin itself, with a semi-translucent black bottle, featuring hot-foiled copper, and a stylised illustration of the loch's legendary monster on the label. The ABV also has a very specific story behind it: the 43.3% the spirit is bottled at reflects the average depth of the loch – 433 feet.

Preferred serve

Loch Ness Spirits have three options to suit non-tonic drinkers and tonic drinkers alike:

(i) Premium tonic with a slice of kiwi fruit.

(ii) Ginger beer with fresh rhubarb.

(iii) Soda water with a split vanilla pod.

Preferred garnish

Kiwi fruit, rhubarb or vanilla pod.

Botanicals

A closely guarded secret.

Recommended cocktail

Ness 75

Ingredients
20ml Loch Ness Gin
2 spoons of spiced apple jelly
15ml fresh lemon juice
Champagne

Method
Pour the gin, jelly and lemon juice into a shaker, shake for several
minutes then strain into a flute and top with Champagne.

30

Kinrara Highland Dry Gin

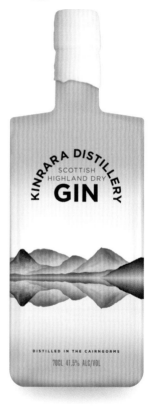

Kinrara Distillery Ltd, Lynwilg Farm Steading, Lynwilg,
Aviemore PH22 1PZ
www.kinraradistillery.com
Price £42.50 / *Quantity* 700ml / *ABV* 41.5%

LYING CLOSE TO the River Spey and the mountaineers' and Munro baggers' paradise that is Aviemore, the scenic backdrop of the Cairngorms National Park and soaring peaks of Ben MacDui provide the inspiration for this newest of gin distilleries.

Sporting one of the best views ever from their front door, Kinrara was built to 'breathe life back into a two-hundred-year-old milking steading' on the Kinrara estate. Founder Stuart McMillan hopes that the new spirits production site will 'build a legacy that will stand for generations' and become known for its exceptionally high quality, handcrafted Highland gins, rums and whiskies. The estate itself offers an expansive range of flora and berries that Kinrara will forage for their gins, mixing them with carefully sourced botanicals from around the globe.

McMillan is keen to champion young talent in the expanding distilling sector and so he hired Heriot-Watt graduate David Wilson, who has a master's degree in Brewing and Distilling, to head up their production team. The distillery is keeping a hands-on approach to the distilling with all of the cut points decided by Wilson using nosing and tasting of the spirit.

Their first gin, Kinrara Highland Dry Gin, has gone down a storm since its launch, and the team has followed up with their second expression, a hibiscus gin, with plans to create other small-batch gins in future. The fledgling brand is also keen to support local charities, and in 2018 donations and support were offered to the Cairngorms Mountain Rescue Team.

There are plans to expand the distillery with a visitor centre to ensure that gin lovers can fully enjoy the Kinrara experience, with Kinrara whisky and rum also set to follow.

Kinrara Highland Dry Gin

Produced on 'Wee Alice', their handmade solid copper pot still from Portugal, with all of the cuts done by taste not yield, Kinrara Highland Dry Gin is described as a juniper-led dry gin, combining foraged and locally sourced botanicals such as rosehips, rowan berries and sweet orange peel.

Floral and sweet, this a great gin, well worth trying either on its own with ice and an orange twist garnish, or mixed with a tonic.

Each batch of two hundred and forty bottles are individually numbered and come with stunning packaging that reflects the glorious scenery that surrounds the distillery, with a striking image depicting the Cairngorms as seen from Loch Morlich.

Preferred serve

Large measure of Kinrara Highland Dry with twice as much Fever-Tree Mediterranean Tonic, lots of ice and a twist of orange peel.

Preferred garnish

A twist of orange peel.

Botanicals

Juniper, coriander, lemon peel, sweet orange peel, liquorice root, angelica root, rosehips and rowan berries.

Scottish Summer

Ingredients
30ml Kinrara Highland Dry Gin
10ml tropical oleo
10ml lime juice
15ml Aperol
Soda

Method
For the oleo: peel your citrus fruit with a knife or peeler, ensuring as much of the white pith is removed as possible. Add the peels to a mason jar and cover with caster sugar, using roughly 50g per lemon as a guide (scale up if using larger fruit). Seal the jar, shake and leave overnight.

The next day, the oil from the peels will have formed a syrup. Add 50ml boiling water per citrus fruit to dissolve the remaining sugar and lengthen the syrup. When all the sugar has been dissolved, remove the peels, bottle and refrigerate for up to a week.

For the cocktail: combine all the ingredients (other than the soda) in a shaker and shake well, strain into a tall glass with ice and top with soda.

Rock Rose

Dunnet Bay Distillers, Dunnet, Thurso, Caithness KW14 8XD
www.dunnetbaydistillers.co.uk
Price £34 / *Quantity* 700ml / *ABV* 41.5%

THE UK'S MOST northerly mainland spirits distillery, Dunnet Bay distillery was launched in 2014 after engineer Martin Murray decided to leave the oil and gas industry to return home to start up a new venture with his wife Claire.

Born of his passion for brewing and distilling, something he had studied as part of his master's degree in Chemical Engineering at Edinburgh's Heriot-Watt University, Martin joined Claire in Caithness in 2011 to plan the distillery they would build there and the spirits that would flow from its stills when it began production. George, the couple's much-loved dog, was involved in the development of the distillery and brand. He is even name-checked on the website as one of the comp-any's founding partners.

Located in the spectacular bay of Dunnet, the distillery is home to their bespoke pot still, Elizabeth, which was designed especially for them and produces the 500-litre batches of their popular Rock Rose Gin. Every bottle of which is filled, hand-waxed, batch-numbered and signed before it leaves their distillery. The small team is firmly rooted in the community, with Caithness residents credited as being brand ambassadors, and family members working at the distillery.

The brand is renowned for their gin range, which includes the original Rock Rose, a Navy Strength and Distillers' Edition and several limited edition seasonal expressions. In addition, they have launched a vodka named Holy Grass – known as bison grass in Poland – for the unusual botanical that was once found on the banks of the River Thurso and which gives it its sweet flavour.

The distillery offers tours (best book in advance), during which you can meet Elizabeth – their still – and see how they produce Rock Rose, sample the gins and visit the shop.

Rock Rose Gin

Named after the 'Rhodiola rosea', the Rock Rose, the original gin released by the distillery, uses the intriguing botanical that grows on the cliffs of Caithness.

The Rhodiola rosea is famed for its health benefits. It's said that the Vikings once sought it out – thanks to its strength- and vitality-giving qualities – and it seems that this fame has lasted into more contemporary times. The first batch of the gin sold out in less than forty-eight hours – an industry record. Interestingly, Martin uses juniper berries from two different countries, Italy and Bulgaria, and both varieties offer specific individual qualities to the final gin.

The recipe for Rock Rose was a long time in the making. Distiller Martin took eighteen months, eighty botanicals and fifty-five experiments to perfect it; the final version uses no less than eighteen botanicals, five of which are grown locally, including sea buckthorn and rowan berries.

But even with all these immaculate details, one of the biggest selling points for Rock Rose is its white ceramic bottle. With its hand-waxed seal and gentle patterns it stands out on any gin shelf.

Preferred serve

Serve with lots of ice in a balloon glass with Fever-Tree Tonic and a curl of orange.

Preferred garnish

A curl of orange or, if you want to try something a little different, garnish with a sprig of rosemary, toasted for full effect.

Botanicals

Juniper, sea buckthorn, Rhodiola rosea, rowan berries, blaeberries, cardamom, coriander seed and verbena, to name but a few.

Recommended cocktail

The Pepperman

Ingredients
50ml Rock Rose Gin
25ml grapefruit juice
12.5ml sugar syrup
Pinch of ground pink peppercorns
Soda
Three strawberries

Method
Take a cocktail shaker, fill the glass half of it with ice and then pour the gin, grapefruit juice and sugar syrup over the ice. Add a pinch of ground pink peppercorns with two strawberries. Shake for several minutes then fill a highball glass with ice. Single-strain the liquor into the glass. Top with soda water and garnish with a strawberry.

Top tips
Keep your eyes peeled for special editions, which use unique botanicals to achieve seasonal flavour profiles; these include Christmas tree spruce tips for 2017's festive gin.

32

Thompson Bros. Organic Highland Gin

Dornoch Distillery, Castle Close, Dornoch IV25 3SD
www.thompsonbrosdistillers.com
Price £32 / *Quantity* 500ml / *ABV* 45.7%

THERE CAN BE few grander settings for a gin distillery than a fifteenth-century Highland castle that is already home to more than a few spirits. Set within the historic seaside town of Dornoch, which lies across the Dornoch Firth from Tain in the heart of North Coast 500 country, Dornoch Castle Hotel is a former bishop's palace turned castle turned hotel.

Owned and run by the Thompson family since June 2000, what was once simply a castle 'haunted' by a sheep rustler is now more famous for the liquid spirits that are poured freely in its hugely popular and award-winning whisky bar. It was in 2015 that brothers Phil and Simon Thompson decided to take the expertise and passion they'd built up behind the bar and follow their dream of opening their own distillery.

Using a one-storey stone shed on the castle grounds that had previously housed a fire station for the local community, the pair launched a crowd-funding drive and eventually installed the versatile distilling equipment which includes a mash tun, wooden washbacks and several copper stills, before producing their first spirit in 2017.

Following lots of experiments with recipes and ratios, gathering essential feedback from the people who helped fund their distillery, the brothers settled on a formula for their Organic Highland Gin.

Uniquely, they use a small percentage of Plumage Archer barley, which is floor-malted, organic and the 'first genetically true barley variety', to make their gin. This links it to the production of their very own single malt, the spirit for which is currently being laid down in casks.

They are also keen to explore the process of how they make their spirits. They say that the long distillation of thirty-six hours that they undertake is key to ensuring every botanical is given time to bed in, helping to create the fullest flavour-journey possible. This patience and care extends to the dilution process with the brothers taking time to add the water gradually so it doesn't have any adverse effect on the spirit.

Having already reached capacity at their current distilling site, Dornoch is set to expand and have launched another crowd-funder in a bid to create a bigger distillery as well as facilities for tourists for who wish to come and see the process in person.

Thompson Bros. Organic Highland Gin

Launched in November 2017, Thompson Bros. Organic Highland Gin is described as having an excellent depth and mouth feel – thanks to the body provided by the malt spirit – with the raspberry and elderflower providing a sweet and floral profile.

Slowly fermented, slowly distilled and slowly diluted to 45.7% ABV, it's a gin with great depth that works as well with mixers as it does in a cocktail. Like the whisky the brothers hope to release in a few years' time, it is perfectly suited for sipping neat or over ice.

Oh, and it comes in one of the coolest bottles you'll find on any gantry or shop shelf.

Preferred serve

Fresh lemon peel, cracked black pepper, served with Fever-Tree Original Tonic Water, though the team say it works just as well neat over ice.

Preferred garnish

Fresh lemon peel and cracked black pepper.

Botanicals

Juniper berries, angelica root, cardamom seeds, aniseed, orange peel, lemon peel, coriander seeds, meadowsweet, elderflower, black peppercorns and freeze-dried raspberries.

Royal Hawaiian

Ingredients
40ml Thompson Bros. Highland Organic Gin
15ml orgeat syrup
10ml lemon juice
25ml fresh pineapple juice

Method
Pour all the ingredients into a cocktail shaker with ice, shake for
thirty seconds and then strain into a chilled coupe glass.

33

Red Door Highland Gin

Benromach Distillery, Invererne Road, Forres IV36 3EB
www.reddoorgin.com
Price £30 / *Quantity* 700ml / *ABV* 45%

I T'S PERHAPS NO surprise that the home town of noted botanist Hugh Falconer would provide the perfect setting for gin making. However, it is surprising that Forres, which is home to two whisky distilleries in the form of Dallas Dhu (sadly now silent) and Benromach, would take so long to have its very own gin.

Located close to the River Findhorn and the Romach Hills, Benromach Distillery is one of the Speyside region's smallest. Built in 1898, the whisky production site was mothballed in 1983 before being acquired by single malt whisky specialists Gordon & MacPhail in 1993, who set about rebuilding the distillery's name, before eventually re-opening in 1998.

Now a hugely popular Scotch brand in its own right – and celebrating its twentieth anniversary this year – the team at the family-owned distillery decided that instead of basking in the success of their massively popular single malt whisky, they'd extend their spirits range to create a gin that reflected the wonderful scenery that surrounds the town.

They spent months working with leading experts in the gin industry to create a gin recipe that would not only appeal to Scottish drinkers but – much like their whisky – would also appeal to drinkers all around the world, ultimately settling on a balanced mix of local and traditional botanicals.

Named after the distinctive red doors at Benromach Distillery, Red Door Gin was launched in July 2018, following the installation of Peggy, a handmade copper still – which is virtually a miniature replica of their spirit still – in the old malt barn at the distillery.

Using a vapour-infused distilling method, and eight botanicals chosen specifically to capture the spirit of Scotland's 'majestic mountains, forests and wind-swept coastline', the London Dry-style gin is designed to be as at home in a personal collection as it is on the gantry in your best-loved gin bar.

Designed to reflect its eponymous red door, the gin comes in a ruby bottle and decorative box with its own sliding door. Also, keep an eye out for images of Scoobie, the distillery's pet cat and mouser.

As a popular tourist attraction, those who visit Benromach to find out more about how this new handcrafted gin is made will soon be able to enjoy a new visitor experience that narrates the story of Red Door Gin and the engaging personalities who create it.

Red Door Highland Gin

A small-batch London Dry gin, Red Door features a strong undercurrent of juniper punctuated with the sweet citrus of the bitter orange and lemon, while the fruity and floral notes of the sea buckthorn and pearls of heather battle it out with the deeper flavours of the rowanberries.

Bottled at 45% ABV, it doesn't betray its stronger alcohol content and works nicely in classic cocktails. It could just as well be enjoyed its own with a few chunky ice cubes and some tart, fresh Scottish raspberries.

We'd expect nothing less from one of the country's most popular up-and-coming spirit producers.

Preferred serve

A chilled balloon glass filled with fresh ice and one part Red Door Gin to two parts good quality tonic. Garnish with fresh raspberries to contrast or with a grapefruit slice to accentuate the botanicals. Stir and enjoy.

Preferred garnish

Fresh raspberries or a grapefruit slice.

Botanicals

Juniper, pearls of heather, coriander seed, sea buckthorn, rowanberry, angelica root, lemon and bitter orange.

Recommended cocktail

The Red Door Negroni

Ingredients
25ml Red Door Highland Gin
25ml Campari
25ml good quality sweet (red) vermouth
Slice of orange to garnish

Method
Take a chilled 'Old Fashioned' glass – a tumbler or whisky
glass is perfect. Take a separate mixing glass with some ice. Stir the
ingredients in the mixing glass and add a little more ice. Strain and
pour over ice in your original 'Old Fashioned' glass and garnish with
an orange slice.

34 Colonsay Gin

Tigh na Uruisg, Upper Kilchattan, Isle of Colonsay PA61 7YR
www.wildthymespirits.com
Price £38.50 / *Quantity* 500ml / *ABV* 47%

HUSBAND AND WIFE team, Finlay and Eileen Geekie, finished their self-build home on Colonsay in April 2016, and moved to the tiny Hebridean island not long after. The pair then founded Wild Thyme Spirits just a few months later. Colonsay Gin was launched in March 2017 and is described as a 'modern interpretation of the classic London Dry style gin' – meaning it's as delectable when sipped neat as it is as the central component of a cocktail.

Finlay explains that they chose to make this traditional style of juniper-led spirit so it would stand out from an increasingly crowded marketplace, which he finds to be 'brimming with flavoured gins infused with unusual botanicals'. Instead, Colonsay would be instantly, sharply recognisable as a gin.

As such, their recipe features botanicals considered typical for a classic London Dry gin, with the exception, of course, of the calamus root, which brings a fiery 'ginger-like rootiness' to Colonsay.

In 2018 the Geekies moved production from Methven to the island and are confident that with the foraging rights they have on the Colonsay Estate, they will create newer expressions that fully show-case the island on which their new distillery is based.

Should any gin aficionado fancy sampling a slice of Colonsay life, then the Wild Thyme Spirits team also offer a 'Gin Lover's Retreat' which includes enjoying the 'remote Hebridean beauty' of the island, the choice of over two hundred gins from around the world, gin cocktails, a tasting and accommodation.

Colonsay Gin

Described as a classic London Dry style gin, Colonsay is a juniper-forward gin, with strong pine notes upfront, followed by an earthy root sweetness.

Coriander seeds lend warmth and depth to the gin, while orange peel brings subtle citrus and calamus offers a kick of fiery ginger. The gin lives on long after the final sip and the lasting finish is that of the sweet roots.

Inspired by Celtic folklore, the bottle's stunning label was created by South African illustrator Caroline Vos and shows the distillery's three 'Brownies' (a Brownie or Uruisg – pronounced 'oor-isk' – in Gaelic was a type of spirit that helped with household chores): ALVA, a delightful, red-haired maiden and twins Doughal and Ferghus, as well as the island that they call home.

Preferred serve

Serve over ice with a premium tonic and a garnish of either orange zest, or, most unusually, a slice of green chilli.

Preferred garnish

Orange zest or a slice of green chilli.

Botanicals

Juniper, angelica root, calamus root, liquorice root, orange peel, orris root and coriander seeds.

Recommended cocktail

Kiloran Waves

Created by Andy Mil from Cocktail Trading Company in London.

Ingredients
50ml Colonsay Gin
1 tsp greengage jam
20ml seaweed and tea syrup*
5ml smoky Scotch (e.g. Ardbeg)
25ml lime juice
1 egg white
Salt, lime and an edible flower to finish

Method
Shake all the ingredients in a cocktail shaker and fine-strain into a cocktail glass. Garnish with a sprinkle of salt on top of the glass, spritz with a twist of lime and decorate with an edible flower.

* To make the syrup
Add 1 tsp loose-leaf breakfast tea, 1 sheet (2.2g) of Nori seaweed and 500g caster sugar to 500ml of hot, not boiling, water. Dissolve the sugar and leave to infuse for ten minutes before straining. This syrup will last in the fridge for two months.

35

Lussa Gin

The Lussa Gin Distillery, The Stables, Ardlussa,
Isle of Jura PA60 7XW
www.lussagin.com
Price £40 / *Quantity* 700ml / *ABV* 42%

THE ISLE OF JURA is famous for many things – its iconic whisky, the Paps and, of course, as the inspirational location in which George Orwell took refuge to write *Nineteen Eighty-Four*. The small island, which lies north of Islay on the west coast of Scotland, now serves as inspiration to three female distillers who are using it as a base for one of the country's newest gins.

In the summer of 2015, self-taught and originally working from a tiny 10-litre still in the kitchen of one of their houses, Alicia MacInnes, Claire Fletcher and Georgina Kitching took their adventurous spirit and love of foraging and used it to create a gin that they describe as a 'distillation of the island'.

Still relatively small-scale – they made only ten thousand bottles in their first two years – the trio all live on Lussa Glen in Ardlussa on the north end of the island, distilling, bottling and labelling the gin themselves.

A true adventurist's gin, Lussa captures not only the island itself but also reflects the environment in which it is nurtured. The trio explore all possibilities in their hunt for the best botanicals, be that rowing out to sea to gather sea lettuce or climbing trees to harvest Scots pine needles.

The botanicals they gather by hand are then frozen rather than dried. And all of the fifteen chosen for the recipe for their aromatic, zesty London Dry gin can either be grown or foraged on the island.

The island's spirit of community means that many Diurach – residents of Jura to you and me – help to produce what's needed: in return for a bottle or two of the finished product, naturally.

Lussa Gin

Using only botanicals that can grow on Jura or be foraged from its hills, bogs, coastline and woods, Lussa Gin features prominent Scottish ingredients such as juniper – which grows wild on the west coast of the island – bog myrtle, Scots pine and rosehip.

As part of Lussa's drive to improve sustainability, the team have started a long-term project to propagate cuttings of Jura juniper and planted five hundred seeds of certified Argyll juniper, as well as growing their own lemon thyme in polytunnels.

The result, distilled on a handcrafted Portuguese copper still – named Jim – is an exceptionally smooth, fresh gin filled with floral notes and slight hints of spice.

Preferred serve

With Walter Gregor's tonic water and a sprig of lemon thyme or mint with a frozen lemon wedge.

Preferred garnish

A sprig of lemon thyme or mint with a frozen lemon wedge instead of an ice cube.

Botanicals

Lemon thyme, coriander seed, rose petals, lemon balm leaves, lime flowers, elder flowers, honeysuckle flowers, bog myrtle, orris root, juniper, water mint leaves, sea lettuce, Scots pine needles, ground elder and rosehip.

Recommended cocktail

Luscious Lussa

Ingredients
50ml Lussa Gin
10ml lime juice
10ml elderflower cordial
3 leaves of lemon balm
1 sprig of lemon thyme
Soda

Method
Muddle all of the ingredients in a tall glass, then fill with ice and top up with soda.

36

Shetland Reel

Saxa Vord Distillery, The Shetland Distillery Company, Unst,
Haroldswick, Shetland Islands ZE2 9EF
www.shetlandreel.com
Price £34 / *Quantity* 700ml / *ABV* 42%

SCOTLAND'S MOST NORTHERLY distillery can be found on its most northern collection of islands. Rugged, remote and beautiful, the island of Unst, Shetland, is the location of the former RAF Saxa Vord base, which now hosts a tourist resort, and is home to the Shetland Distillery Company.

Launched in 2014 by two couples, Debbie and Frank Strang and Wilma and Stuart Nickerson, the company is a blending of both couples' desires to launch a new distillery on the island. The Strangs played a major role in the revival of Saxa Vord after the RAF left, and Nickerson is an industry veteran who had previously revived the Glenglassaugh Distillery in Aberdeenshire before selling it to the BenRiach group.

The quartet now distils all of their gins on the island. They make sure that each one has a distinct link to the island, the unique location of which means that the most northerly of distilleries is also the most easterly and the most remote. In fact, it is closer to Bergen in Norway than to Aberdeen and closer to the Arctic Circle than it is to London.

Launched initially with both gin and whisky in mind, the distillery debuted with Shetland Reel, which was inspired by the island. This was followed up with Ocean Sent, in honour of the seas around Unst, and Simmer Gin, created in celebration of Shetland's famously drawn-out summer twilight, which has the delightful local name of 'Simmer Dim'.

In celebration of the island's culture and rich ties to the past, the team also created a selection of small-batch, cask-aged, Navy Strength Up Helly Aa gins to celebrate the infamous Shetland fire festival and pay homage to the island's connection to the Vikings.

Whisky, as can be expected with Nickerson's past, will eventually play a part in the distillery's production cycle. To highlight this they produce a blended malt Scotch. Blended for them on the mainland, this is then shipped to the distillery where it's reduced to bottle strength with local water and bottled.

Each recipe for the gins goes through a three-stage process. It's first developed in a small glass still, before being perfected in a small copper still, then finally produced on the full-size still. Each gin has a signature ingredient that ties it to Unst. In the case of the Ocean Sent, its bladderwrack seaweed is harvested from the shoreline, while the original Shetland Reel uses locally harvested apple mint.

Shetland Reel

Created to provide a unique snapshot of the island on which it is made, Shetland Reel original gin features nine key botanicals. The most important of which – other than the juniper – is the apple mint, sourced from the Unst market garden and dried before being added to more traditional ingredients like coriander seeds, angelica root and citrus peel. This creates a gin that's traditional in style but has a citrus sweet flavour and refreshing yet subtle notes of mint.

Preferred serve

Mix with Fever-Tree Original and serve in rocks glass with plenty of ice.

Preferred garnish

A wedge of pink grapefruit, sprigs of mint and of lavender.

Botanicals

Juniper, coriander, angelica root, orris root, cassia bark, almond powder, orange peel, lemon peel and apple mint.

Shetland Southside

Ingredients
50ml Shetland Reel
25ml pink grapefruit juice
10ml simple syrup
10ml lemon juice
6–8 mint leaves
Soda
Grapefruit rind to garnish
Sprig of mint to garnish

Method
Muddle the mint and gin together in a shaker, add the remaining ingredients, top with ice and shake until cold. Double-strain into a tall glass filled with ice and top up with soda. Garnish with grapefruit rind and a mint sprig.

The Botanist

Bruichladdich Distillery, Isle of Islay PA49 7UN
www.thebotanist.com
Price £34 / *Quantity* 700ml / *ABV* 46%

FOUNDED IN 1881 on the Hebridean island of Islay by three brothers – William, Robert and John Gourlay – Bruichladdich (pronounced 'Broo-k-lad-dee') distillery has suffered mixed fortunes over the years. It was considered state-of-the-art when it was built, but in 1994 it was eventually mothballed.

Wine merchant Mark Renyier's decision in December 2000 to buy the neglected production site was certainly a good one. But the real stroke of genius was his decision to poach industry legend Jim McEwan from Bowmore.

It was Jim's idea to expand production to include white spirits and in 2012, after much consultation with local botanists, Islay-based Richard and Mavis Gulliver, the first batch of the Botanist gin went on sale.

The product of many years of research and adaptation of the distillation techniques already employed to make whisky, the Botanist uses twenty-two botanicals that are locally sourced and hand-foraged. The gin's name is not just a play on words as the link between the team and their botanicals is key to the product's ongoing success. Professional forager, James Donaldson, helps to source the plants from the hills, shores and bogs of this Hebridean island.

These botanicals have not only been chosen for the flavour they impart but also for the fact that they are readily available and are in 'plentiful supply', thereby protecting Islay's delicate environment.

Jim McEwan then perfected this recipe on a Lomond still – charmingly dubbed Ugly Betty – which had been rescued from the old Inverleven Distillery in Dumbarton and transported to the island by barge. Since then, the Botanist has gone on to become one of the most successful of all Scottish gins, and in 2018 it's outselling Bruichladdich's own whiskies.

The Botanist

The first thing you'll notice about the Botanist is its eye-catching bottle, which features the Latin names of all thirty-one of its botanicals. Yes, you read that right. Thirty-one.

Twenty-two of these are locally foraged including apple mint, chamomile, creeping thistle, gorse, bog myrtle, heather and hawthorn. These are then added to nine traditional botanicals, including coriander, angelica and cassia bark, as well as the juniper to create, as expected, a rich and complex gin.

Described as having a 'mellow taste with a citrus freshness', the Botanist is one of the most versatile Scottish gins and, as the producers are keen to point out, is perfect for experimenting with. Have some fun with it!

Preferred serve

Experimentation is best when it comes to enjoying this gin.

Preferred garnish

Try adding some thyme and lemon balm, fresh rosemary picked from the garden or a sprig of mint.

Botanicals

Apple mint, chamomile, creeping thistle, downy birch, elder, gorse, hawthorn, heather, juniper, lady's bedstraw, lemon balm, meadowsweet, mugwort, red clover, spearmint, sweet cicely, bog myrtle, tansy, water mint, white clover, wild thyme, wood sage, orange peel, orris root, lemon peel, liquorice root, juniper berries, coriander, angelica, cinnamon and cassia bark.

The Botanist Collins

Ingredients
50ml The Botanist Gin
20ml lemon juice
25ml cloudy apple juice
10ml elderflower cordial
Soda
Apple fan to garnish

Method
Add all the ingredients in a highball glass with ice, top with soda
and garnish with an apple fan.

Kirkjuvagr

The Orkney Distillery and Visitor Centre, Ayre Road,
Kirkwall, Orkney KW15 1QX
www.orkneydistilling.com
Price £39.95 / *Quantity* 700ml / *ABV* 43%

HAVING PREVIOUSLY BEEN home to two world-famous whisky distilleries and a hugely popular brewery, Orkney has recently embraced the world of modern Scottish spirits in a big way. The past few years have seen the introduction of several award-winning gins and even a rum.

One of the most prominent of these is the Orkney Distilling Company, which was founded in January 2016 by husband and wife team Stephen and Aly Kemp, and whose first product is the tongue-twisting Kirkjuvagr Gin – pronounced 'kirk-u-vaar'.

Created following a long period of working with consultants on research and experimentation, Kirkjuvagr's recipe was inspired by a local legend that spoke of a variety of angelica brought to the islands by Scandinavian seafarers centuries ago. Still found growing wild on the Orkney island of Westray, this angelica was chosen as one of the defining botanicals in a recipe featuring other local botanicals, including ramanas rose, burnet rose and borage, as well as that most Orcadian of ingredients, traditional bere barley.

Each of these Orcadian botanicals are specially grown or handpicked for the Orkney Distillery by the Agronomy Institute of the University of the Highlands and Islands, at their site overlooking Kirkwall Bay. They have even developed a strain of calamondin oranges to add a kick of citrus to the signature gin.

Originally contract distilled at Strathearn Distillery in Perthshire, the production of Kirkjuvagr and its sister gin Arkh-Angell (Storm Strength Edition – 57%) moved home in 2018 to the island's main town. There you'll find the company's bespoke distillery and visitor centre on the harbour front, featuring a coffee shop as well as a gin bar.

This remarkable facility is the perfect excuse for any gin fan to visit the island; it offers a Gin Making Experience where fans of the Orcadian spirit can spend all day at this unique distillery, learning the secrets of crafting their own gin on a miniature still and receiving a bottle to take home with them.

The Orkney Distillery is also home to a third gin: the lighter, sweeter Harpa. This is a tribute to the arrival of spring and the 'advantages that longer nights and the fairer weather of summer-time bring', as celebrated by the island's Norse ancestors.

Kirkjuvagr Gin

Keen to retain a connection to Orkney's Viking heritage, the Orkney Distillery chose 'Kirkjuvagr' for the name of their gin. It's the Norse word for 'Church Bay' – the thousand-year-old Viking name for their home town of Kirkwall – and reflects the distillery's stellar setting and the home of those ancient seafarers who claimed the islands in their own name in those pre-medieval days.

A modern gin that's 'quite simply, unmistakably Orcadian', Kirkjuvagr is a complex spirit with notes of sweetness, salt and spice all following the initial floral hit.

The packaging features the rolling waves of the seas around Orkney and the Vegvisir, or Viking compass, reinforcing that strong connection with the Norse seafaring tradition. Should you be looking for a novel way to dispense Kirkjuvagr, the team sell their own handcrafted gin dispensing taps. What could be better?

Preferred serve

Over ice with your favourite tonic, garnished with orange peel.

Preferred garnish

Orange peel.

Botanicals

Juniper, angelica root, aronia berries, borage, cassia bark, coriander seed, holy thistle, lemon peel, liquorice root, marshmallow root, milk thistle, nutmeg powder, orange peel, orris root powder, rose hips (ramanas and burnet rose), calamus root, heather flowers and finally some bere barley.

Recommended cocktail

The Pamplemousse

Ingredients
35ml Kirkjuvagr
25ml Pamplemousse (grapefruit liqueur)
50ml pink grapefruit juice
Dash of grapefruit bitters
Sugar syrup to taste
Dehydrated pink grapefruit to garnish

Method
Mix the ingredients together and pour into a coupe glass, then garnish with the pink grapefruit.

39 Sea Glass Gin

Deerness Distillery Ltd, Newhall, Deerness, Orkney KW17 2QJ
www.deernessdistillery.com
Price £34 / *Quantity* 700ml / *ABV* 43%

THE RUGGED BEAUTY of Scotland's islands is complemented by their wonderful natural larders and the entrepreneurial spirit of a people who have no choice but to look beyond the ready availability of items found in the big cities of the mainland.

Head north to Orkney and the north-eastern coast of the main island and you'll find one of the country's most thrilling new producers. Launched in 2017, Deerness Distillery aimed to expand the island's distilling scene from the production of a globally renowned single malt whisky at Highland Park and Scapa, to an exciting range of craft spirits such as gin, vodka and, incredibly, small-batch rum.

Founded by Stuart and Adelle Brown, Deerness is the first new distillery on Orkney for one hundred and thirty years. The family-run business produced its first spirits – Sea Glass Gin and Into the Wild Vodka – on their three Portuguese copper alembic stills, which are named Walt, Zing and Matilda.

Construction of this innovative new site began in 2016 with six gins originally produced before they launched a year later. Each of the six were put to the taste test before Sea Glass was chosen as the flagship juniper spirit.

With plans to expand their site to be more inclusive for tourists, the Brown family hopes to establish a shop and tasting room on site and are also looking at creating a polytunnel system that will allow them to grow five out of seven of their botanicals on site in a bid to protect the environment of this wild, spectacular island.

Sea Glass Gin

Named for the glass found while combing the island's exhilarating beaches, Sea Glass Gin is unique for a few reasons. The first new gin to be solely distilled on the island of Orkney, it is made using tarragon instead of coriander, which founder Stuart believes brings a smoother flavour and gives their gin a truly distinctive profile.

Cut with pure Orcadian water, Sea Glass is made on Matilda – the family's gin still – and is described as tasting of spices, citrus and juniper.

Preferred serve

Serve a Sea Glass G&T with ice and Franklin & Sons tonic water.

Preferred garnish

Blueberries or a slice of kiwi.

Botanicals

Juniper, cucumber, mint, lavender, lemon verbena leaf and tarragon.

Recommended cocktail

The Sea Pink Cocktail

Ingredients
45ml Sea Glass Gin
15ml Into the Wild Vodka
Crushed ice
45ml blueberry juice
45ml Franklin & Sons tonic water
Blueberries and lemon rind to garnish

Method
Coat the rim of a 150ml martini glass with lemon juice and sugar.
Mix all the ingredients together and garnish with blueberries and a
lemon rind spiral.

Misty Isle Gin

The Distillery, Hillfoot, Viewfield Road, Portree,
Isle of Skye IV51 9ES
www.isleofskyedistillers.com
Price £34 / *Quantity* 700ml / *ABV* 41.5%

CONSIDERED ONE OF the country's most beautiful regions, the west coast island of Skye is home to some truly spectacular and dramatic scenery. From its waterfalls and fairy pools to rock formations such as the Quiraing and the Storr, it enjoys phenomenal popularity with everyone from tourists to film directors.

Famous for restaurants such as The Three Chimneys and Kinloch Lodge and, of course, its world-renowned whisky distillery, Talisker, the island's food and drink scene has undergone a dramatic boom with the addition of two new spirits production sites – a new whisky distillery, Torabhaig, has popped up at Teangue while Skye's first gin distillery has opened at Portree.

Built in the back garden of a home that's been in the family for five generations, Isle of Skye Distillers aims to share the 'spirit of Skye' with the world. Brothers Thomas and Alistair Wilson – Skye born and raised – combined their experience in the building trade and hospitality industry to launch their distillery in February 2017.

All of their gin is produced on their four copper stills, Chursty, Mairi, Euan and Finlay, while bottling and labelling is done by hand on site.

The distillery is still very much a family affair – the Wilsons alone work to produce their line of gins. This includes Misty Isle Gin, Tommy's Gin – the recipe for which involves poppy seeds – and seasonal expressions such as the Mulled Christmas Gin, which uses all of the ingredients for a mulled wine, soaked in Amarone red wine before distillation.

Misty Isle Gin

Misty Isle Gin derives its name from the island's epithet and is designed to reflect Skye's stunning landscape, with the Old Man of Storr and the Cuillin mountain range offering particular inspiration.

This can be seen on the bottle itself: the label design and its multiple raised edges reflects the breathtaking mountains that form the island's backdrop, while the copper foiling gives a nod to their two original stills, Chursty and Mairi.

The gin itself combines the crystal-clear spring waters from the Storr Lochs with botanicals foraged on Skye. The balance of botanicals, with its hand-sourced juniper from Skye's wild places, means that Misty Isle is described as a juniper-heavy gin. It has an earthy mix of angelica root, liquorice root and orris root, with a good portion of citrus (lemon) and some spice from coriander and black cubebs as well as an intriguingly 'secret ingredient' picked at high altitude on Skye.

Preferred serve

Misty Isle should be served with a slice of orange peel and Scottish tonic, but mint lemonade makes a nice alternative to tonic. Another good serve is with a cinnamon stick and ginger ale.

Preferred garnish

Orange peel, or a cinnamon stick.

Botanicals

Juniper, orris root, liquorice root, black cubebs, coriander, grains of paradise, lemon peel, lemon verbena, cassia bark, angelica root and a secret Skye botanical.

Recommended cocktail

Shepherd's Delight

Ingredients
50ml Misty Isle Gin
25ml elderflower liqueur
25ml strawberry liqueur
Rose lemonade
Orange peel to garnish

Method
Mix all the ingredients apart from the lemonade, shake over crushed ice and top with the rose lemonade and garnish with a twist of orange peel.

Isle of Harris Gin

Isle of Harris Distillers, Tarbert, Isle of Harris HS3 3DJ
www.harrisdistillery.com
Price £37 / *Quantity* 700ml / *ABV* 45%

THE LAST BASTION of land before you hit thousands of miles of the Atlantic on the way to Newfoundland in Canada is a breathtaking, rugged place like no other. Isolated and ethereal, it's perhaps not where you'd expect to find a gin distillery.

Described as Scotland's first social distillery, the Isle of Harris Distillers lies where North and South Harris meet and is only the second spirits production site to be found on the Outer Hebrides. It was built as part of a project to create production and tourism jobs for Harris and its community, and also to help stop population decline on an island that's arguably one of Europe's most beautiful.

With whisky the main target of the new spirits production site, few could have imagined how successful the gin, initially conceived as a keepsake for tourists to buy at the distillery, would become.

Created using hand-dived sugar kelp, on their small copper gin still, known affectionately as The Dottach after 'a similarly fiery and feisty local woman', the gin comes in a bottle that's sure to be one of the prettiest you'll come across: wave-like patterns are etched upon its aqua blue glass in tribute to its coastal home and the seas of Luskentyre. Each bottle is created with deliberate imperfections to make it easier to hold while pouring – this imaginative, meticulous team really have thought of everything.

The bottles feature a simple wood and cork stopper and are sealed with the coordinates of the distillery's location; so popular are these uniquely rippled bottles that the distillery had to introduce a rationing system in 2016 when the specialist Yorkshire factory that makes them struggled to keep up with demand.

As a personal touch, each bottle is sent directly from the Isle of Harris along with a 'thank you' message.

Isle of Harris Gin

Isle of Harris Gin – launched in 2015 – was the distillery's first gin. In its creation a consultant botanist selected sugar kelp, an ingredient popular in Japanese cookery, ahead of other island plants such as heather and bog myrtle.

The dry kelp brings a saltiness to the final spirit, but also, surprisingly, a sweet flavour. Managing director Simon Erlanger points out that the distillery only uses small quantities of the kelp, as its flavour can be very powerful.

Sweet and spicy, with a slight hint of that wonderful sea air, Isle of Harris is an enigmatic gin that is more than worthy of the attention heaped upon it.

Preferred serve

In a tall glass with several large cubes of ice, add a splash of a premium tonic (Walter Gregor's Scottish tonic is the in-house recommendation), and garnish with a wedge of red grapefruit.

Add a few drops of the distillery's own Sugar Kelp Aromatic Water if you really want to take this G&T to the next level.

Preferred garnish

Red grapefruit.

Botanicals

Hand-harvested sugar kelp, Macedonian juniper berries, English coriander seed, cubebs (Javan pepper), bitter orange peel, angelica root, cassia bark, orris root and liquorice.

Recommended cocktail

The Caper Ceilidh

Ingredients
60ml Isle of Harris Gin
12.5ml Dolin Blanc Vermouth de Chambery
2 drops of pink grapefruit-infused saline solution
Caperberry brine
Red grapefruit to garnish
Three caperberries to garnish

Method
Make the grapefruit saline solution by soaking the zest of a red grapefruit in a simple saline solution (20mg salt to 80ml water). Chill a coupe glass with ice. Add 12.5ml of the vermouth to a mixing glass with ice. Stir, then strain off and discard the vermouth. Add 60ml of gin to the vermouth-rinsed mixing glass and ice. Add 5ml caperberry brine, and two drops of grapefruit saline solution. Stir the contents to chill thoroughly. Fine-strain into the chilled coupe glass. Serve with a garnish of three caperberries and a twist of red grapefruit.

Persie Zesty Citrus Gin

Persie Distillery, Auchenflower, Glenshee Road,
Bridge of Cally PH10 7LQ
www.persiedistillery .com
Price £29 / *Quantity* 500ml / *ABV* 42%

LYING JUST SOUTH of the borders of the Cairngorms National Park in the quiet setting of Glenshee and the rolling agricultural land of Perthshire, is where you'll find Persie Distillery. What began as a simple gin tasting on World Gin Day in June 2014 has grown to become a hugely successful distillery with not one but three core gins.

The idea for the distillery sprung forth while founder and Institute of Brewing and Distilling graduate Simon Fairclough was touring the country with Gin Club Scotland, helping not just Scots but also gin fans around the UK to find their 'perfect snifter'. Taking up residence in the former Persie Hotel at the foot of Glenshee in Perthshire, Simon set about turning the discoveries he had made about gin understandings and preferences into a physical product in a bid to give consumers what they want.

The Persie team created three core gins, each designed with the Scottish gin palate in mind and reflecting the three favourite gin profiles of gin drinkers in Scotland – fruity, savoury and sweet – just as Simon learned during his travels.

Launched in May 2016, the distillery has become a permanent fixture at gin events nationwide and their aromatic gins are handmade in small batches in a bespoke 230-litre copper pot still. They are made using water sourced directly from the local hills surrounding Glenshee, a place traditionally – and poetically – known as the glen of fairies.

Persie is unique in that it approaches gin from not only the angle of taste and production styles but also, and more significantly for them, of aromas. Simon explains that the customer feedback they received showed that a great gin needs more than just a great taste: it needs to stimulate an individual's sense of smell.

Persie Zesty Citrus Gin

The three gins that Persie have created are made with carefully chosen botanicals to evoke an emotive and comforting scent. Zesty Citrus is described as sharply fruity, chock-full of limes and oranges; Herby & Aromatic is dry and savoury, with rosemary and basil; and Sweet & Nutty Old Tom is full-bodied and creamy, with fresh vanilla pods, almonds and a hint of root ginger.

The Zesty Citrus is described as a 'burst of limes and blood oranges on the nose, with a sharp citrus cut-through and long, zingy finish'. It is the perfect gin for those looking for fruitier flavours both on the nose and on the palate.

It takes around two hundred fresh limes and oranges to create each small batch of roughly three hundred bottles, which means that this gloriously summery gin offers exactly what it says on the label.

Preferred serve

Serve as a G&T with full-fat or elderflower tonic, and garnish with lime and torn mint.

Preferred garnish

Lime and torn mint.

Botanicals

Juniper, freshly zested limes and oranges.

Recommended cocktail

The Hugo

Ingredients
2 measures Persie Zesty Citrus Gin
1 measure elderflower cordial
A few leaves of fresh mint
Champagne or Prosecco
Mint or elderflower to garnish

Method
Put the mint, elderflower cordial and gin into a cocktail shaker. Add ice and give it a good shake. Double-strain into a champagne flute, filling to about halfway up. Top up with Champagne or Prosecco. Garnish with some mint leaves or elderflowers.

43

Heather Rose Gin

Strathearn Distillery, Bachilton Farm Steading,
Methven, Perth PH1 3QX
www.strathearndistillery.com
Price £36 / *Quantity* 700ml / *ABV* 40%

LYING CLOSE TO the village of Methven in Perthshire, you'll find a remarkable little distillery that produces a range of handcrafted spirits and is easily one of Scotland's most industrious producers.

Located in the rich agricultural land surrounding Perth, Strathearn Distillery is home to several types of gin, a single malt whisky and a golden Scottish rum. Founded in 2013 by Tony Reeman-Clark, it's become a hub of activity with many of Scotland's smaller gin producers beginning their distilling journey here under the team's expert tutelage.

Tony and his team have launched four core gin expressions, with the classic small-batch gin being closely followed by the Oaked Highland Gin. Described by Tony as the point where whisky meets gin, this expression is a pretty gold colour and is designed to be enjoyed as an 'after dinner' gin. The subtle oakiness provided by the staves from American oak barrels gives it a really rich, intriguing flavour.

Keen to offer a lively selection of great flavours, Strathearn also created their Citrus Gin with botanicals such as Italian lemons, Spanish grapefruit and Kaffir lime leaves. A personal favourite from their range is the Heather Rose Gin. Each of their expressions is handcrafted and small-batch; each batch produces two hundred and eighty bottles.

Keen to support other fledgling distillers, Strathearn have teamed up with local producers to create Arbuckle's Honeyberry Gin, using the 'grape of the north'. Created in conjunction with local farmers, Arbuckle's, this outstanding gin sees honeyberry added as a botanical. Once distilled, it is blended with fresh unpasteurised honeyberry juice, which gives it a powerful flavour and distinctive purple colour.

The distillery's original goal was always to create single malt whisky. Tony explains that he set up what is 'probably the smallest distillery in Scotland' after getting into whisky 'almost by accident' after curiosity about cut points and the production techniques of single malts got the better of him.

With the private cask club launched and plenty of his spirit maturing, the distiller is on course to create his own successful single malt whisky brand – bottle #001 of which sold for £4,150 – and he plans to expand the distillery to a new site in the near future.

Heather Rose Gin

This intriguing gin begins life in Strathearn's copper pot stills with the delicate rose and heather flowers added post-distillation to ensure they survive the process so their unique flavour is added to the gin. Tony explains that the original idea was to filter out the colour, but when tonic water was added in one of their first tastings, the colour changed to a delicate pink blush – and it was decided that the colour should remain.

Floral and sweet and with a hint of spice, Heather Rose can be enjoyed neat over ice or with a mixer.

Preferred serve

Serve in a champagne flute with a chilled tonic and nothing else. A lighter flavoured tonic is good, but the gin is bold enough to use almost any tonic. Drop in a raspberry if you must have a garnish.

Preferred garnish

A sweet fresh raspberry.

Botanicals

Juniper, coriander seeds, orange peel, lemon peel, liquorice root, rose petals and purple heather flowers.

Bramble Rose

Ingredients
50ml Heather Rose Gin
25ml lemon juice
10ml cane sugar syrup
10ml rose water
10ml crème de mûre
Lemon and brambles to garnish

Method
Shake the first four ingredients over ice, then strain into a rocks glass filled with crushed ice. To finish, pour the crème de mûre slowly over the top of the drink to bleed through the ice. Garnish with lemon and a fresh bramble.

McQueen Gin

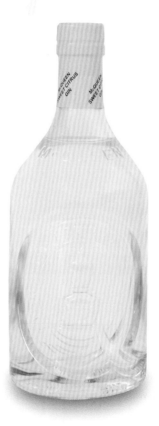

Trossachs Distillery Limited, The Barn,
Upper Drumbane, Callander FK17 8LR
www.mcqueengin.co.uk
Price £33 / *Quantity* 500ml / *ABV* 42%

AS YOU HEAD north from Glasgow and Stirling, you'll find the Perthshire town of Callander, which abuts the soaring peaks and gorgeous lochs of Loch Lomond and the Trossachs National Park. Situated close to the River Teith, Callander is also home to a unique gin distillery, which was launched in June 2016 by chartered mechanical engineer Dale McQueen and his wife and business partner Vicky, a retired chef.

Tired of the daily grind, in the summer of 2015 the pair decided to leave their more conventional jobs and set up a distillery. As Dale tells it, he called his boss the next morning to resign then flew to Germany the week after to order the still, at which point, the McQueens still had no building to put it in or so much as a licence to use it.

But from there, what would become the Trossachs Distillery, slowly began to take shape. Self-taught in distilling, the McQueens turned their expertise in flavour and analytics to create one hundred and fifty iterations of gin over a six-month period. Then, taking in detailed feedback from around three thousand members of the public, their core range began to emerge.

To their surprise, they found that they had most success by diverging from the tried-and-tested formula of traditional flavours. Instead they embarked on a path that would lead to them building a stable of gins that included some 'world first flavour expressions' such as Sweet Citrus, Smokey Chilli, Spiced Chocolate Orange, Mocha and Chocolate Mint.

The pair are keen to point out that, despite their distinctive profiles, this selection of expressions does not include flavoured gins created with post-distillation additions, but rather they are made in the traditional manner with everything happening during distillation and only water added post-process. Each expression is a crystal-clear liquid, a full 42% ABV and, vitally, tastes predominantly like gin.

And they haven't stopped there. As well as a Super Premium dry gin, they have created a range of custom gins for specific customers such as Chocolate Cherry, Scottish Raspberry with White Chocolate, Vanilla Rose and Double Juniper and Peppercorn.

This popularity and overwhelming demand meant they outgrew their current distillery in just eighteen months. Now the McQueens are looking to create an extension to their current set-up so as to increase capacity tenfold.

Smokey Chilli Gin

According to the McQueen website, Dale is a bit of chilli fan so it's no surprise that a flavour profile such as this would feature in their range. For me, it's the one in their collection of distinctive flavours that I find the most intriguing. Containing no less than three types of chilli, you'd expect it to be intense in its flavour with a lot of full-on heat, but surprisingly – or perhaps unsurprisingly given that it's made with the chilli added before distillation – it is actually a lot more subtle, with a deep smoke reminiscent of mezcal, with hints of spice and a backdrop of juniper.

Each of the McQueen gins was originally bottled in striking blue ceramic with different coloured wax tops, but in 2018 the decision was made to change to a more eco-friendly glass bottle.

Preferred serve

Serve 50ml McQueen Smokey Chilli Gin, 100ml Fever-Tree Ginger Beer and a sliver of green or red chilli in a glass with loads of ice and garnished with a grapefruit spiral.

Preferred garnish

A grapefruit spiral.

Botanicals

Bulgarian juniper, chipotle chilli, smoked chilli, chilli and lime.

Recommended cocktail

The Smokey Chilli Negroni

Ingredients
50ml McQueen Smokey Chilli Gin
50ml sweet vermouth
50ml Campari
Ice
Orange peel to garnish
Chilli slice to garnish

Method
Add the ingredients to a cocktail shaker and shake until cold to the touch. Strain into an ice-filled glass and garnish with orange peel and a chilli slice.

Teasmith

Contract distilled at: Strathearn Distillery, Bachilton Farm Steading, Methven, Perth, PH1 3QX

www.teasmithgin.com

Price £38.95 / *Quantity* 700ml / *ABV* 43%

IN THE CURRENT boom for Scottish gins, it can be hard to find a USP that allows you to really stand out from the crowd. However, with Aberdeenshire-based company Teasmith you have the first, and what is believed to be the only, gin distilled in Scotland (currently produced by Perthshire's Strathearn) that uses handpicked tea as one of its key botanicals. Sourced from the Amba Estate in Sri Lanka, the special Ceylon tea was chosen as a key botanical thanks to the citrus notes and distinctive minty sweetness it provides when distilled.

The Teasmith also reflects the area's rich and largely unknown heritage links with the tea trade, with Aberdeen harbour being famous for its shipbuilding of old, with several notable tea clippers being built there. However, it's the story of James Taylor from Auchenblae, near Laurencekirk, who is the gin's true inspiration. As a young man in 1815, he left Aberdeenshire and headed for Sri Lanka, which at the time was a coffee-growing nation called British Ceylon. The island's crop was suffering extensively from crop disease.

Taylor had heard about the success of tea growing in India and decided to create the island's first commercial tea plantation. It was so successful that the island soon switched to tea growing. Taylor set the wheels in motion that have helped turn Sri Lanka into one of the most significant tea-growing regions in the world. To this day, Taylor is revered as the 'Father of Ceylon Tea'.

Working with tea consultant Beverly Wainwright to source the hand-picked and hand-rolled tea from Sri Lanka, Nick and Emma Smalley from Udny Green, began formulating the idea for a gin in May 2015. After sixteen months of experimenting and forming the brand, they launched Teasmith Gin in December 2016 – with the first batch of five hundred and seventy bottles selling out in just a week.

The Teasmith has a very classic flavour profile with a strong juniper profile backed up by citrus notes and a refreshingly sweet finish.

Preferred serve

Use copious amounts of ice, a premium tonic and a sprig of fresh mint for a really crisp and refreshing G&T.

Equally, it is often said that the gin is very smooth neat – the sweetness of the tea as it rounds the profile means you can enjoy it simply over ice on its own or with a mint leaf or two.

Preferred garnish

Fresh mint leaves – the Teasmith team find these really accentuate the mint flavour tones that the tea provides when distilled. If you don't have mint to hand, a simple lemon peel twist also works really nicely.

Botanicals

Juniper, coriander seed, Ceylon tea, dried orange peel, rose petals, orris root, angelica root, liquorice root, honeyberry, grains of paradise and calamus root.

Recommended cocktail

The Classic Southside

The simplicity of the ingredients and the predominant citrus and mint flavours, with their slight sweetness, mean this cocktail marries exactly with the spirit's flavour profile.

Ingredients
60ml Teasmith Gin
30ml fresh lime juice
15ml sugar syrup
8 mint leaves
Champagne
Sprig of mint to garnish

Method
Add all the ingredients to a cocktail shaker with plenty of ice. Shake vigorously and fine-strain into a long champagne flute. Top up with a splash of Champagne for a touch of fizz and garnish with a small sprig of mint.

46 Raven Gin

Contract distilled at: Deeside Distillery, The Steading,
Lochton of Leys, Banchory AB31 5QB
www.ravengin.com
Price £35 / *Quantity* 500ml / *ABV* 45%

ABERDEENSHIRE'S WELLSPRING OF great gins shows no signs of running dry and the inventiveness and entrepreneurial spirit rife in the region has given rise to yet another excellent gin in the form of Raven Gin.

Created by brothers Callum and Peter Sim who, after attending and organising spirits events over the years through Peter's consultancy firm Peaty Nose, decided that together they could produce something unique and exciting. The result is Thought and Memory, named for Huginn and Muninn who were the Norse God Odin's twin ravens. This delightfully well-balanced gin is made using six carefully selected botanicals including the subtly sweet citrus fruit mandarin.

As part of the launch, the brothers also created the 'Founder's Edition', a stronger, more intense version of Thought and Memory that's taken from the very first distillation run and will be limited to around three hundred bottles.

Future plans include the addition to the range of a stronger 'military grade' gin of around 57% ABV.

Fresh on the nose, light and smooth on the palate, with a distinctive warm and slightly spicy finish, the unmistakable sweet notes of the mandarin are carried throughout Thought and Memory.

The stylish bottle, replete with the eponymous ravens, is offset by copper styling on the lettering, wax top and cork, to reflect the slow distillation involved in the gin's creation.

Preferred serve

Over ice with a light tonic and garnish of lemon.

Preferred garnish

A slice of lemon.

Botanicals

Juniper, angelica, cassia, coriander, cubeb pepper and mandarin.

Mandarin MojitJa

Ingredients
50ml Raven Gin 'Thought and Memory'
100ml Fever-Tree Sicilian Lemonade
7 mint leaves
½ unpeeled mandarin, chopped
10ml sugar syrup

Method
Add the mint and mandarin to a heavy-based rock glass and pour over
the sugar syrup. Muddle the mint and mandarin and fill the glass with
ice. Pour over the Raven Gin, top with the lemonade. Garnish with
mint leaves and mandarin.

47

Garden Shed Gin

Cuckoo distilled at: Eden Mill Distillery, Main Street, Guardbridge,
St Andrews KY16 0UU
www.thegardensheddrinksco.com
Price £40 / *Quantity* 700ml / *ABV* 45%

AS IF TO highlight just how accessible the gin scene is now, the Garden Shed Drinks Company was set up by two Glaswegian couples, well, in their garden shed. Upon returning home from London, Scottish international rugby union player Ruaridh Jackson and team-mate Ryan Grant, along with their wives Kirstin and Maxine, hit upon the idea to create their own gin using botanicals sourced in their back garden in Scotstoun, alongside one or two more traditional ones of course.

After a few experiments with different recipes, they settled upon one they found appealing and, enlisting the knowledge of the Eden Mill Distillery team – a partnership bred of the St Andrews brand's sponsorship of Jackson and Grant's Glasgow Warriors team – they began cuckoo distilling (that is, distilled using Eden Mill's equipment) Garden Shed Gin.

Made using fourteen selected botanicals, including brambles and dandelion root (sourced at home) along with juniper, grains of paradise and lavender, the gin is bottled in rustic packaging to reflect the nature of its origins. Kirstin and Maxine provide the creative input here with a bottle designed with a rustic feel furnished with wooden tags and twine.

The provenance of their product and the sustainability of the ingredients they use are hugely important to the quartet. Some of the profits from the sale of the gin are donated to charities such as Trees4Scotland and the Bumblebee Conservation Trust.

With its sweet and citrus notes, this is a well-balanced gin that's dangerously drinkable, even on its own.

Preferred serve

In a glass with plenty of ice, Fever-Tree Original Tonic and garnished with blackberries and a sprig of rosemary.

Preferred garnish

Blackberries and a sprig of rosemary.

Botanicals

Juniper, blackberries, dandelion root, bay leaves, liquorice root, elderberries, grains of paradise and lavender.

Recommended cocktail

The Grunting Growler

Ingredients
50ml Garden Shed Gin
1/3 of a can of ShinDigger Mango Unchained IPA (or other sweet IPA)
A few dashes of passionfruit juice
A few dashes of yuzu juice

Method
Pour the gin into a tall glass filled with the IPA, then add the dashes of
passion fruit and yuzu juices.

48

Gin Bothy Gunshot

Gin Bothy, Brechin Road, Kirriemuir DD8 4LH
www.ginbothy.co.uk
Price £36 / *Quantity* 700ml / *ABV* 37.5%

KIM CAMERON WILL be the first to admit that the Gin Bothy concept was created by accident when, following her original idea to enter a homemade jam into the World Jampionships in Perthshire in 2013, she discovered she had a surplus of fruit juice.

A family member suggested she should use it to create a gin. Kim's first attempt – made with a seventeenth-century recipe – soon overtook the popularity of the jam and she quickly realised she was onto something with real potential. Kim decided to use a traditional method to create her gins, and so she makes small batches steeped in fruit, and hand-turned daily to infuse, with sugar and a few secret ingredients added.

The gin producer's first release was her Bothy Original gin, which is infused with botanicals including locally grown heather, milk thistle, hawthorn root and rosemary, as well as pine needles from the Loch Arkaig forest near Spean Bridge.

Founded more recently, Gin Bothy Gunshot Gin is handmade in batches of thirty-eight bottles at a time. It's named after one of Scotland's oldest sports – shooting – and boasts a warming mixture of cinnamon, cloves and spices.

Kim explained that it was originally created for a party of shooters, who said they were after a tipple that would give them a much-needed 'inner glow' on the freezing cold moor and that also matched the colour of their bullets. Warming and filled with spiced notes, Gunshot is a savoury gin that's best enjoyed 'by the campfire'.

Keen to preserve bothy culture, Kim is also a fan of sustainability and has struck up a partnership with the Woodland Trust. This helps to raise funds to restore Loch Arkaig pine forest by donating £1 from every bottle sold.

Preferred serve

Best served neat over some ice. Adding ginger ale and a slice of orange will enhance the warmth of the cinnamon.

Preferred garnish

A slice of orange.

Botanicals

Juniper, cinnamon, cloves and spices.

The Smoking Gun

Ingredients
50ml Gin Bothy Gunshot
1 dash of demerara syrup
3 dashes of Angostura bitters
2 dashes of orange bitters
Cinnamon stick and orange peel to finish

Method
Add the ingredients to a Boston shaker with ice and shake well. Sieve through a strainer. Serve with a cinnamon stick wrapped in orange peel. Light the cinnamon stick for extra effect.

49 Stirling Gin

Contract distilled at: Glasgow Distillery Company, Deanside Road, Glasgow G52 4XB (production is moving to a new Stirling distillery in 2018)

www.stirlinggin.co.uk

Price £34. / *Quantity* 700ml / *ABV* 43%

THE HISTORIC CITY of Stirling is famous for its iconic landmarks such as its castle and, of course, the Wallace monument but, other than the nearby Deanston whisky distillery and the lost Craigend Distillery, it's been bereft of any form of spirit producer for centuries.

However, Cameron and June McCann, the husband and wife team behind the popular Stirling Gin brand are hoping to change that when they finally bring distilling back with the opening of a distillery and visitor centre in the shadow of Stirling Castle late in 2018.

Their Stirling Gin, which began its life in a tiny copper pot still in the McCanns' Bridge of Allan kitchen in 2015, has grown to become one of Scotland's most popular gins. Moving its production back to Stirling also marks a return to the couple's home town.

Handcrafted and small-batch, this distinctive gin derives its idiosyncratic herbal notes from a combination of basil and Stirlingshire nettles, with the early season nettles providing a slight sweetness of note, which enhances the taste and tickles the palate in a unique manner.

The nettles are hand-foraged from two historical locations that are intrinsically linked with the history of Scotland's medieval royal capital. The Minewood is still home to the medieval copper mine that was once used to produce currency for the Stewart kings of Scotland and is a rich source for nettles.

The rolling green parkland of the King's Park, which was used for hunting by the Stewarts under the glowering watch of Stirling Castle's towering walls, is now the producer's other favoured foraging ground for the Stirlingshire nettle.

Preferred serve

A combination of ice and Fever-Tree Mediterranean Tonic, garnished with basil leaf and orange peel.

Preferred garnish

Basil leaf and orange peel.

Botanicals

Angelica root, juniper, lemon peel, orange peel, basil and Stirlingshire nettles.

The Bloody Scotland

This drink was created exclusively as the signature cocktail of Scotland's international crime writing festival of the same name.

Ingredients
50ml Stirling Gin
Dash of blood orange sour syrup
Dash of lime juice
Cranberries
Soda

Method
'Lovingly pour over ice and top up with soda water to provide a striking visual appearance that's reminiscent of a blood-red setting sun and has a taste just as memorable.'

50 Ginerosity

Contract distilled at: Pickering's Gin Distillery, 1 Summerhall, Summerhall Distillery, Edinburgh EH9 1PL

www.ginerosity.com

Price £25 / *Quantity* 500ml / *ABV* 40%

D RINK GIN AND do good – a simple message but one that works for what is considered to be the world's first social enterprise gin.

Chris Thewlis, social enterprise pioneer and founder of the Beer for Good chain, teamed up with Marcus Pickering and Matthew Gammell, founders of Pickering's Gin, and together they partnered with the charity Challenges Worldwide to create Ginerosity in October 2016. The aim was to raise funds to help young adults from disadvantaged backgrounds, not just in Scotland but also further afield.

The gin itself was designed by the team at Pickering's to incorporate ten ethically sourced botanicals to create a spirit that's full of character and as appealing to drink as it is altruistic in its intent. It's fresh, light and bold, with citrus and juniper giving way to sweetness, and a subtle hint of peppery spice and a crisp dry finish.

Preferred serve

For a generous G&T, serve 50ml Ginerosity with Fever-Tree Original Tonic in a highball glass with cubed ice and a garnish of mint leaves.

Preferred garnish

Mint leaves.

Botanicals

Juniper, lemon, lime, angelica, cardamom, heather, lemon myrtle, coriander, orange and cloves.

Recommended cocktail

The Southside

As warmer weather threatened to make an appearance, the sun-loving team at Harry's Southside created this summertime cocktail especially for Ginerosity. It balances its citrus-forward notes with the bright sweetness of the soft fruits.

Ingredients
50ml Ginerosity
25ml lime juice
20ml gomme syrup
Dash of bitters
Fresh mint leaves

Method
Best shaken and served over ice, with a garnish of mint leaves.

Image Credits

Acknowledgements

Writing a book isn't easy and it would have been even harder without the help and support of the following people (in addition to my publishers and their infinite patience). With thanks to:

Julia Fletcher Smith, for being my anchor and keeping me grounded when I felt overwhelmed, for always offering a word of encouragement, and being on hand to share the occasional gin with me.

My mum for providing me with a love of reading and writing, my dad for giving me the confidence to speak to people about their passions, and my stepdad for always being there with a beer.

Stephen White and Alison Higgins of the Scottish Gin Society, for being a ready source of information (particularly your excellent website), and for support of this industry.

Dave Broom, for being a gin guru and taking the time to chat even when he was on holiday on Islay.

Jamie Shields at the Summerhall Drinks Lab, for listening to my crazy requests, offering advice and helping me get my head around the stranger cocktail terminologies.

Jonathan Engels, for unravelling the world of Scottish juniper for me and teaching me why so few Scottish producers can use it sustainably.

The guys at Porters Gin, who I wasn't able to include, but who were complete gentlemen about it.

Blair Bowman, for being out there posing the question of what actually constitutes a Scottish gin, and driving the debate forward.

Geraldine Coates, for politely putting up with my pestering.

David and Marjorie Smith, for advice and for plenty of opportunities to enjoy a gin or two.

Kirsty Black, for chat about distilling, flavours and botanicals.

And, finally, to all the producers included in *Gin Galore*. Without you, this fledgling industry would be nothing, so thank you for making it what it is and for producing your amazing gins.